W9-BOF-834

TEACHING BASIC OBEDIENCE:
TRAIN THE OWNER,
TRAIN THE DOG

Alexandra Powe Allred

Printed and Distributed by T.F.H. Publications, Inc
Neptune City, NJ

TEACHING BASIC OBEDIENCE:
TRAIN THE OWNER, TRAIN THE DOG

Alexandra Powe Allred

For Tasha, my Dobie, the reason I got into dog training.

T.F.H. Publications, Inc.
One TFH Plaza
Third and Union Avenues
Neptune City, NJ 07753

Copyright © 2001 by T.F.H. Publications, Inc.

All rights reserved. No part of this publication may be reproduced, stored, or transmitted in any form, or by any means electronic, mechanical or otherwise, without written permission from T.F.H. Publications, except where permitted by law. Requests for permission or further information should be directed to the above address.

This book has been published with the intent to provide accurate and authoritative information in regard to the subject matter within. While every precaution has been taken in preparation of this book, the publisher and author assume no responsibility for errors or omissions. Neither is any liability assumed for damages resulting from the use of the information herein.

ISBN 0-7938-0524-4

If you purchased this book without a cover you should be aware that this book is stolen. It was reported as unsold and destroyed to the publisher and neither the author nor the publisher has received any payment for this "stripped book."

Printed and bound in the United States of America

CONTENTS

INTRODUCTION

W hen word came down that Elizabeth Dole, Director of the Department of Transportation at the time, was inquiring about training for her dog, the office was abuzz. I was a full-time dog trainer for the Olde Towne School for Dogs in Alexandria, Virginia. It was not that uncommon for us to train celebrities' and politicians' pooches. As always, we wondered what kind of dog Dole had and who would be best suited to work with that dog. We all had specialties. It turned out to be Dole's personal secretary who was interested in training, but everyone was anxious to work with owner and dog just the same.

Every trainer was bidding for this near-celebrity-status dog. I should have been suspicious when I—so new to the training world—was given the assignment. I had trained a string of really well-tempered dogs and owners in comparsion to some of my colleagues. It had been a blissful few months. I should have known, as all good trainers do, that this streak would have to end.

I arranged to meet with the owner and dog for a consultation, as is my policy, before we began training. It is merely a formality. The idea is to make sure the dog is suitable for training and that the owner is up for the task at hand. But I was cocky then, and there was no doubt in my mind that I could train any dog who came my way—no matter how grand the problem.

I was undaunted by a telephone conversation I'd had with the dog's owner. "I'm not sure he's trainable," Ms. W. had said. "I'm not sure he can be trained." "Of course he can be trained," I had said. "He's not too old?" she asked hesitantly. "No dog is too old to learn a new trick," said I. "Well, and he's a little. . . slow. I mean, he doesn't pick up on things very quickly. I'm afraid you might lose patience with him." I laughed at the thought. Patience is my middle name.

Then, I met Gus. I had been behind the counter, pulling all the appropriate paperwork, when Gus entered. A Golden Retriever was doing a down/stay in the middle of the room, and a Cocker Spaniel was sitting quietly while her owner sampled some collars against her glossy coat. Having just come from a grooming appointment, the Cocker was bathed, combed, and sporting blue ribbons in each ear. The room was quiet and calm. Until Gus entered.

The front door opened, and Gus dragged Ms. W. across the room toward the dogs. He bounced on top of the Golden, deliriously happy to have made a new friend. The Golden was up in a flash ready to play, the trainer was yelling, "No! Down! Stay!," but Gus was off! Within seconds, he was on top of the Cocker, and she was not nearly as receptive as the Golden. Fur was flying, owners were scrambling around trying to grab leashes, and trainers were spilling out of the woodwork. By the time the dogs were separated, the Cocker's ears were encrusted in slobber and the blue ribbon hung from Gus's mouth. Gus smiled brilliantly. He had made two friends.

I looked back over my shoulder at my smiling boss. Gus, it turned out, was a three-year-old male Doberman Pinscher, that had been born retarded. He was crossed-eyed and had a twitch that caused him to throw out his front legs in spasms. His ears remained uncut, big elephant ears falling in his face, making him look like a goofy hound dog. He spit the bow out and lunged at me, smiling all the time.

"He's. . . he's a little slow," Ms. W. said again. "He doesn't understand that not everyone wants to be his friend." I leaned forward and took hold of the leash while Ms. W. struggled to unwrap herself. "That's why we're here. I really want to keep him, but he's got to learn how to walk on a leash. Do you think he can?" Gus was smiling. My boss was smiling. And now other trainers were smiling. What could I say? I had a reputation to protect. I had to try.

Ms. W. and I agreed that Gus would learn four commands: heel, sit, down, and stay. We would use a six-foot nylon lead, a nylon collar (because the chain made him nervous), and a two-week trial period. Gus would come to school every day, Monday through Friday, for two weeks, and stay all day with me. The contract was signed, we shook hands, and I waved goodbye to them as Gus dragged Ms. W. down the street. Then, I turned to face the smirks and prophecies of failure by my colleagues. I bet a week's paycheck I could train Gus, and spent the rest of the day saying, "You'll see," and wondering how I was going to make it without a paycheck.

Monday came, and I was ready. I stood outside the school, awaiting their arrival. At 8 a.m., Gus and I said goodbye to his mother and headed out for our first walk before any of the other trainers could lay eyes on him. Or me. I would let Gus run out to the end of the lead, give him a slight tug and tell him, "No, stay with me," and pat my side. Most pups become suspicious after a few tugs and begin watching the handler. Eventually, they fall back next to the handler's side so the two may walk in harmony. But Gus had a better idea. Once he hit the end of the lead, it occurred to him that he should then quickly turn and charge me at full speed. I found myself buckling at the knees and covering myself for protection, while he bodyslammed me.

Eventually, he grew tired of this exercise and began to quietly trot back in my general direction. By late afternoon, sweaty, exhausted and covered with bruises, I led Gus back toward the school in a heel. What usually takes other dogs 20 minutes to learn had taken three hours. But we did it. The sit command was the next lesson, but I needed a break.

The first hour on Tuesday was spent reminding Gus that I was not to be charged when he hit the end of the lead. I planted myself in front of a law office to give him a review of Monday's lesson. Some of the leading trainers in this country will tell you not to chew out the dog because he can't understand what you are saying. I know this and always give proper commands and praise. But by Tuesday afternoon, everyone inside the law office could hear, "Hey! Hello? What are you doing? What do you think yesterday was all about? Hey! Are you listening to me?"

I decided to introduce the sit, stay, and down commands on Tuesday and spend the rest of the week reviewing. Repetition was going to be the only way to communicate with Gus. Sitting involved pulling the nylon lead high behind his ears with my right hand, while pushing down on his bottom with my left hand. It was easy enough to get him to sit, but getting him to stay there was another matter. I found that by holding his collar steady and crouching over him, barely touching his back, I essentially blocked him into place. The position was torture on my knees and leg muscles. But there the two of us sat in front of the law office, staring out into traffic, as I said "Stay, stay, stay, stay, good stay," so many times I thought I might lose my mind. The only time I stopped talking was to smile politely at the lawyers' clientele while I squatted over the dog. The down involved lying on top of Gus, pinning him to the ground, and repeating my soothing, pleasant commands of "Stay, stay, stay, good stay."

For much of Wednesday and Thursday, I either squatted over or lay on top of Gus in front of the law offices. All pride was gone. There was a paycheck on the line here. By Friday, most of the staff at the law office were surprised to see Gus sitting and lying alone. Although I stood very close to him, he was no longer pinned. He was staying on his own!

The following Monday started off with Gus hitting the end of the lead, turning, pouncing on me, and giving me more of a kiss than I cared to have. The thought of ringing his little neck sprang to mind, but I knew it would do no good. Losing my temper with him would only turn our lesson into a game. We spent another 20 minutes reviewing, while I worked on my patience. I made sure my tones were pleasant, but firm.

For the next three days, we practiced all his commands over and over again. Gus spent most of each day with me; he even had lunch with me, doing down/stays. He had come a long way, but I was still worried. We only had two more days and this dog still couldn't heel without tripping both of us. The problem was this: He would begin heeling with me very nicely, but would suddenly and spasmatically jerk his front right leg out to the side, sticking it under my foot. I would, not seeing it, step on his foot and he would let out a loud seal-like roar that caused everyone within earshot to turn toward the source of the noise. I tried switching sides, altering my gait, and even walking bowlegged so that my knee would jut out and push him farther from my body. Nothing worked. Gus grasped the concept of sitting, staying, and lying down, but the foot thing was a real problem. I tried everything. I high collared him. I jabbed him in the ribs with my knee to move him over. I argued very loudly with him.

Finally, we got it. For the next two days, Gus and I heeled back and forth in front of the law office, much to the amusement of the staff. Our heeling was perfect. Gus was lined up on my left side. His shoulder was flush against my left leg, his chest bone not much farther ahead than my shin bones. His head was up. There was a comfortable slack in the lead indicating that I was not holding him back nor was he straining at the lead. He was paying attention to me, comfortable, and heeling beautifully. No one driving by would have ever known he was slow or how much we had struggled to come this far. They would have noticed only the person handling him.

Head tilted so I could watch him carefully, I walked along the sidewalk, dragging my left foot. My foot was turned out, toes facing Gus, so that there was no way he could slip his paw beneath it. To do this, I had to lean out to the right, watching his gait. As I said, he looked perfect. I looked like the Hunchback of Notre Dame, limping along beside him. Occasionally, Gus would throw his foot out, but it would only cause me to stumble slightly. Gus barely knew what happened. Eventually, he began to walk straight, since my foot prevented him from throwing the foot to the right.

We continued with the sit, down, and stay commands, and his owner signed him up for another week just to polish his skills. Interestingly, as Gus's confidence began to build, the spasms practically went away. Puppy self-esteem is extremely important, as you will see over and over again in the following stories, and obedience training is the sure-fire way to build it.

Ms. W. gushed about how bright her boy was after all, how wonderful he had become, and what a good trainer I was. The truth was that I had become Gus' student. He had reminded me how important repetition is, and he taught me that a true partnership must be built on just that—a partnership. As embarrassing as it was, once I was willing to change my style of walking, we were able to work on his. All too often, people expect animals to make all the changes for us. We hope to train them and have them behave like robots, forgetting they are individuals. The perfect partnership means give and take on both sides.

As for the bet: I won! On the last day I saw Gus, we were going through our paces in front of the law firm when one of its employees passed us. He smiled when he saw Gus's improvement. "I would have bet a paycheck that he was never going to get the hang of it." "Don't worry," I told him. "Someone already did."

HOW TO USE THIS MANUAL

Whether you are the proud parent of a new puppy or the exhausted parent of an adult dog in dire need of manners, let's get started. (Even those of you with an adult dog should read over the puppy training section of the book. It will give you a better feel for what is to come and also let you see how much training you already might have done.)

After you begin the training, you should refer to the book to recognize any behavioral problems that your pup may have. Read about properly correcting your dog, dealing with submissive wetting, barking, or growling, or any problems your pup may be having. The idea is to familiarize yourself with behavioral problems while you are training so that unanticipated problems won't sneak up on you.

Perhaps the single most important thing I hope you will learn from this book is patience. Sadly, we live in a world that has a fast-paced, "fast-food" mentality, from wanting to get our

Training is a two-way street and should ultimately help to form a relationship with your dog that is based on trust, confidence, and respect. Author Alexandra Powe Allred with her prize students.

fries quickly to wanting our dogs trained quickly. There are gadgets on the market such as shock collars that are horribly overused because we want fast results. In all my years of training, I have only known one dog that truly needed a shock collar for training. She was a Basset Hound with her own set of problems. And while most of the eight trainers at the dog school disliked the shock collar, we all agreed that in this one case, it could save her life.

But for the vast majority of dogs, the shock collar is entirely inappropriate. I have seen far too many dogs on shock collars that had no business being on one. But owners were impatient, wanted fast results, and weren't really interested in building a relationship of give and take. In fact, in the city where I now reside, animal behavioralists at Ohio State University, area vets, and I are painfully aware of a particular trainer abusing this method. I became aware of the guy when I saw an Airedale in my neighborhood being trained on the collar. My interest was instantly piqued. An Airedale on shock? I was curious what his problem could be. I would later find out there was no problem. He was a sweet, docile, lovable fellow, and a typical Airedale. Translation: powerful, playful, and full of the dickens when he wanted to be. Without being rude about my fellow trainer, I warned these people about the "quick fix" syndrome. I warned them about a trainer—any trainer—so quick to put a dog with this kind of temperament on the shock. I warned them that they would not have the respect and admiration of their Airedale, Cody, after this kind of abuse.

Approximately five weeks after the training was completed, Cody's people were ready to try my way of training. No surprise, Cody was blowing them off. Patience will earn you a tremendous friend, guard dog, and family member. Quick fixes will not.

I think you will find solace—while you struggle to train your pooch—in reading true and funny stories about what other owners have gone through in their training. And you will find solutions to any particular problems your pooch may have, as well as the tricks he will try to play on you. In short, I want to tell you all the things that Fido didn't tell you (and didn't plan to tell you).

Part One

PICKING A DOG

I NEVER THOUGHT OF THAT...

IMAGE IS EVERYTHING!

Why do you want the breed you want? Have you chosen the dog as a status symbol? This is an important question because, so often, in cases like these, the pup is the loser. German Shepherds and Dobermans are extremely sensitive, sweet dogs, but how many people get one hoping for or expecting a mean, protective dog? Because these dogs are so intelligent and sensitive, it does not take much to turn them into aggressive, unstable dogs. Yet, when we let them be what they want to be, which means true to their natures, we find that Shepherds and Dobermans have gotten a bum rap.

One of my very good puppy students was a young Pit Bull named Levi. He was very handsome and so sweet. All the trainers loved him. He did all of his commands perfectly, interacted beautifully with the other dogs, and even resisted all kinds of temptations I threw his way. He just held up his beautiful square head and squinted his sweet eyes at me. Levi knew he was being set up, and he loved it because he knew I would praise him and give him lots of attention when he succeeded.

So, it was a surprise when his owner called and asked to meet with me. "We have a problem," he said. I couldn't imagine what it was; Levi was in every way perfect. At lunchtime, Mr. M. came in while Levi gnawed on a doggy biscuit I had given him. I asked Mr. M. to have a seat and wondered what was on his mind. I still remember his exact words. "I think I have a lemon." "Excuse me?" I said. Mr. M. replied, "A dud, a lemon." He pointed to Levi. He wanted Levi to be aggressive, the stereotypical bloodthirsty Pit Bull that Levi was never meant to be. Truth be known, Pits are another breed that have gotten a bad rap. Yes, certainly, Pit Bulls have an aggressive instinct. But unless trained to be killers, Pits are very sweet. Every one I have ever met was incredibly cute and cuddly, with the exception of one. With that particular Pit, I got to see firsthand how very fast, ferocious, and terrifying they can be.

Why would you want this? I leaned forward and took the bone from Levi. He looked up at me and licked his chops, hoping to get it back. "You see," said Mr. M., "He doesn't get mad at anything." Very gently, I shoved Mr. M. as Levi watched. I did it a few more times until Levi was quite distressed. Quietly, he gave me a low growl ("Cut that out, please!"). I obliged, explaining to Mr. M. that the dog's protective nature was there and would show itself if need be. Mr. M. left feeling very happy, but he left me wondering why anyone would want a ticking time bomb and questioning what was in store for my sweet, little Levi.

In New York, during the summer of 1997, an elderly man died of a heart attack while trying to rescue his Schnauzer from a Pit Bull, a teenage boy fell to his death from a roof top while fleeing a Pit Bull, and a little girl was badly mauled. New York's Mayor Rudolph Giuliani and the Housing Authority planned to launch anti-Pit Bull regulations, calling Pits "vicious and menacing" animals. But animal advocates point out, and rightly so, that many Pits are dear family pets and that many Cocker Spaniels and Chihuahuas are far more aggressive. Truth be told, during the 1980s, I was bitten more by Cockers than any other breed. The difference, however, is that Pit Bulls have the frightening ability to carry out terrible damage with their incredibly powerful jaws and bodies. In the inner city, Pit Bulls are status symbols of toughness, and they are trained to be aggressive.

With large breeds, size is often very important to people. As far as Dobermans go, Kaiser is one of the largest, most majestic-looking Dobies I've had the privilege to meet. As a lean pup, he weighed 100 pounds and was not done

No matter what their size, all dogs need proper training in order for them to become well-mannered members of the family.

growing. His father, Conan, was a very muscular 115 pounds. (Both are exceptionally large Dobermans.) One day, while I stood on the sidewalk holding Kaiser's leash, a man walked up and asked about him. People always did. The man told me that he had a Dobie that weighed 160 pounds. (Believe it or not, this happened frequently when I was with Kaiser.) Really? *A 160-pound Doberman?* Do you fly him overhead at the Macy's Day Parade? At 160 pounds, the only way that Dobie would be moving around would be on a gurney. But, it is very common for people to size each other up by their dogs. As I write this, you can't see me, but I am shaking my head. *It never has made sense to me.*

There is also the flip side. There are a lot of people who get very small dogs for social status. They aren't looking for companions—they are looking for cute little toys. It's no surprise that these are the dogs who never learn to walk on a leash because they are carried everywhere for the first three years of their lives. Then, when their owners get tired of carrying them, they are irritated to discover their little Fifi has no intention of walking on a leash.

Having said all of this, there are people who do choose breeds for their specific qualities. Many older, less-active people choose breeds compatible to their lifestyles. Sugar and Spice, two Tea Cup Poodles, were properly trained and loved from the start. Together, they weighed six pounds sopping wet. Because of their small size, their owners were able to take them everywhere with them, and they

Every breed has a certain image or reputation; however, each dog is an individual and should be treated as such.

truly loved and appreciated the dogs' true Tea Cup qualities, just as US diver, Greg Louganis, relished the majestic, powerful qualities of his Great Danes.

Before you choose a breed, ask yourself what it is you want in a dog. Determine what qualities you are looking for and make a list of breeds that fit the bill. When I found Nala, I was looking for a pup who could tolerate two active young girls. I needed a dog who could withstand teasing and ear pulling. He had to be big enough to hold his own and possess protective and fun-loving qualities to grow up with my children. Nala, a female we found at the animal shelter, is a Shepherd/Boxer mix and she fit the bill.

ARE YOU READY FOR A DOG?

If you have not yet picked out a puppy—chances are, you already have—I feel compelled to share a few things you may not have thought of. Your dog would want it that way.

A friend of mine, Janet, struggled with the destructive behavior of her dog, Heidi. They lived in a small two-story townhouse with no backyard. Ouch! This was not a good start. But wait—cute "little" Heidi is a Norwegian Elkhound. The breed was developed to hunt elk and loves vast unconfined areas. This is not a dog intended to be confined to small quarters. It is understandable, then, that this puppy was destroying things in the house.

You need to make sure that every member of the family is willing to take responsibility for a dog before bringing him into the household.

Another client was at wit's end with his Lakeland Terrier, Planty. Lakeland Terriers are small, weighing about 15 pounds. They are originally from England where they are used to hunt fox and badgers in their dens. These energetic dogs are stubborn, active, and spirited. They are very good at burrowing down into small holes—and they love to burrow away. Now, Planty was an incredibly sweet and affectionate Lakeland Terrier, but (no surprise) he loved to try to dig up the carpeting in his home. We were able to break him of this habit, but it was long and frustrating work, because it was in his nature to burrow.

You can see that it is very difficult for these breeds to understand that they have done something wrong when they are only doing what comes naturally to them. Behavioral traits that are in the nature of the pup can be very difficult to discourage.

You also need to consider the size of the animal and its living quarters. Size, however, may be misleading. Do not assume that all small dogs will do well in an apartment or that all large dogs needs lots of running room. For example, Jack Russell Terriers and Beagles are two small dog breeds that need lots of running room, and the Neapolitan Mastiff is a large dog that is adaptable to living in an apartment—as long as there is a strong person willing to take him on long walks twice a day. There are some breeds (some of the Greyhound breeds, for example) that are not suited to apartment life because they need a great deal of daily

Puppies are adorable, but they also are a lot of work. If you do not have the time to devote to a young pup, an older dog may be for you.

exercise. All dogs need regular exercise.

Larry and Shelly are a very active couple. Both of them work long, hard hours, but they also own a sailboat and love the outdoors. A few years ago, they bought two Golden Retrievers, Barnum and Bailey. They have taught their dogs to ride in the boat (and wear life jackets). They have also trained them in basic obedience and spend a great deal of time with them. The result is two happy, well-behaved Goldens and two very happy, seemingly well-behaved people.

In addition to where and how you live, it is also important to consider timing in purchasing a pet. Many people like to get a puppy as a gift for their children, friend, or relative during the holidays, but this can be extremely traumatic for a pup and terribly inconvenient for you and the recipient. The holidays can be very hectic and may generate too much activity for a young pup that was once used to a cozy, familiar den shared with his littermates. Suddenly, the little pup is surrounded by excited children and the chaos of visiting relatives. Housetraining at this time can be very difficult. It is always a better idea to wait for a calmer period in your life to consider getting a pet. If you are determined to get a puppy for your loved one, consider getting a picture of the pup with some puppy essentials. Explain that once the holidays are over, your loved one can pick up the puppy from the shelter or the breeder.

In addition, each dog breed is represented by a national breed club. Specific clubs can provide you with literature about the breed, as well as a list of breeders in your area and nationwide. These clubs may be contacted through the American Kennel Club, 260 Madison Avenue, New York, New York, 10016. Often, the names and addresses of the secretaries of breed clubs may be found in *Dog World* and *Dog Fancy* magazines. Keep in mind, though, that as helpful as these organizations may be, they are naturally biased toward their own breeds.

Years ago, I overheard a Samoyed breeder tell a client that they are stable, loving animals that adore children and are excellent watchdogs. This is true. However, they are also very stubborn and can prove to be a real challenge during training. One of my clients was a 70-year-old woman who used a walker to get around. Images of her training a sled dog were scary.

And who ever told Nancy Reagan to get a Bouvier? I still wonder about that. Why didn't the person just suggest that she take up bobsledding? It came as no surprise to the dog training community when Lucky was quietly sent to the family ranch. I've always been a "the glass is half full" kind of gal, but Nancy Reagan had about as much of a chance controlling a Bouvier puppy as I had of escaping Eubie, the 180-pound wonder Dane, unharmed. And in both cases, the human should have known better.

I had agreed to watch Eubie, a fellow trainer's pup, while he was out of town. Eubie, a 180-pound Great Dane puppy, had a real confidence problem. He was very afraid of most things and, through training, we were trying to build his confidence. I had let Eubie go outside, and after some time I went out to get him. Dusk had fallen, and Eubie bravely stood out there alone, sniffing the air. I made a noise to let him know I was there. No response. So, I walked up behind him and quietly said, "Boo!" He ran off, tail tucked between his legs, yelping so loudly the neighbors probably thought the tornado siren had gone off. I, of course, being sensitive to Eubie's feelings, burst out laughing. Eubie stopped, turned, and saw that it was me. He was so relieved that it was not some mad Great Dane serial killer that he charged happily toward me. I was too busy laughing to see this. It had rained the night before, and the ground was very soft. I think to this day there is probably a permanent imprint of my body on the ground where I was slammed down after Eubie jumped on my chest.

I have made many unwise decisions in my dog training career. Just as the guy

Do your homework and research the different breeds to ensure that you choose the dog that best suits your lifestyle.

who instructed Nancy Reagan to get a Bouvier regrets his decision, I truly regret saying "Boo" to a skittish Great Dane puppy. Ah, well, I digress. . . The point is that you have to know which questions to ask when considering a specific breed. You also have to seriously examine the answers. For example, ask if it is known to be a stubborn breed and the breeder may say, "Well, I wouldn't say stubborn, maybe headstrong." It means the same thing. If you are short on patience or have little time to devote to training, stay away from that one! Ask if the breed is good with children. If you are told that these dogs are a little "shy" or "leery" of children and you have a child, choose another breed. Ask questions that are relevant to your needs and lifestyle.

It is very important that you also ask yourself several other questions before adopting a puppy. Do you really have time to devote to a pet? How often do you travel? Could you take your pet with you? Who will take care of your pet when you have to work late or when you are away?

While I was in college, I missed out on dorm life because I had dogs. Unlike most of the other kids, I could not just take off for spring break or go away for weekends. I had to make plans weeks in advance, and most often I would not go anywhere unless I could take the dogs. For me, it was more fun when my dogs were around. For other people, this might be considered a great inconvenience.

Do you have a yard? Many apartment complexes that allow pets very often have 25-35 pound weight limits. Some complexes that allow pets offer a dog walk area, but many do not. If you do not have a yard, are you prepared to walk your dog? Even when it is six o'clock in the morning and freezing outside? Even when you have the flu? Are you up for packing a pooper-scooper? If your answers are "No," then you should probably put off getting a puppy until your lifestyle changes.

DOGS AND CHILDREN

First and foremost, you must teach your children to respect dogs. While being an ear-pulling-resistant pet was a requirement for my dog, Nala, that is not to say that I allow my girls to pull ears and tails. We have had many long talks about treating Nala with respect, but they are little girls and I know there will be "incidents." I have taught them that dogs are not toys and that not all dogs are friendly. Indeed, many dog bites occur because children do not know they should not tease or approach strange dogs.

Dog ownership helps to teach your child respect for animals.

I was pleased during my most recent trip to the park when a little girl approached me and asked if my dogs were friendly. When I said yes, she then asked both her mother and me if she could pet the dogs. Her mother said, "Okay. But, remember to put out your hand." And the little girl gently and slowly placed her hand out, palm downward, so that Sosi and Nala could sniff her. Of course, the only danger she faced from those two was to be kissed, but it was good to see that she was already learning how to properly approach strange dogs.

Between one and three million dog attacks occur annually in the United States. According to the Centers for Disease Control, half of all American children will be bitten by the time they are 12 years old. They will be bitten by their family's dog or a neighbor's dog. Little girls between the ages of two and four are the most bitten group of people, because they tend to walk right up to dogs' faces.

There are several rules you can teach your children about proper behavior around dogs that should help them to avoid being bitten:

- Never put your hand through the window of a parked car to pet a dog.
- Never put your hand through a fence to pet a dog. Dogs will always protect their territory, whether it is their home, yard, or car.
- Always ask the owner of a dog for permission to pet him. If the owner is not around, leave the dog alone.
- *Never* tease a dog.
- Never go into someone else's yard to retrieve a ball.
- Never play near a yard in which a dog seems agitated. Again, dogs are protective of what they perceive as their areas.
- Always greet a new dog with your hand facing down, stretched out, so that the dog can smell you first (after you have gotten permission from the owner).
- Never yell or jump around strange dogs. And absolutely no hugging around a dog's neck! No matter how sweet the canine, this makes some pooches nervous.
- Never run away from a dog. Even a nonaggressive dog will chase someone running away from him.

Having said all this about teaching your children, you still must be cautious about the breed you pick. Many parents are tempted to get smaller breeds believing that a smaller dog will be less likely to hurt the children. This is not necessarily so. I cannot tell you how many times I have had a family come in for

Children may unintentionally injure or frighten a smaller dog. Be selective and make sure to teach your child how to handle your dog gently.

training because their small dog had bitten the kids. Smaller breeds are often more temperamental because they can be more easily hurt than larger breeds. Often, child's play can get too rough, and the smaller breeds will snap to warn children to get away.

There are exceptions. Jack Russell Terriers and Beagles, for example, have excellent reputations with children. I grew up with a Beagle mix and "tortured" her endlessly. I stuffed her in doll carriages, forced her into baby clothing, pulled her ears, taunted her with her own food. . . never once did she even growl. Yorkshire Terriers, Silky Terriers, Lhaso Apsos, and Maltese are other breeds noted to be good with children, but they are classified in the canine world as "Toys." Toy breeds can be very delicate physically, and a rough child could easily provoke them to bite. Had I grown up with a Toy, I'm sure I would be riddled with well-deserved scars.

If you want a smaller breed and you have children, be selective. Talk to your vet. Pick a few breeds that are appealing to you, and do some research. Most importantly, take an honest look at your child or children. Are they rough? Loud? Or do they play quietly? My sister could easily have had a Tea Cup Poodle, but I needed a Saint Bernard. I always recommend a mixed breed from the shelter. It is hard to go wrong with a shelter puppy, especially a Labrador mix. Every dog is different, and it is important to research the breed in which you are interested.

An energetic puppy makes a great playmate for a child and vice versa. With the proper training and supervision, they are bound to become the best of friends.

If you are considering a larger breed, again you must think about your lifestyle and family. Not just any large breed will do. There are several large breeds that are more aggressive or temperamental than others. If your child is very active or loud, I would recommend staying away from hyper, more active breeds. For example, Boxers are wonderful with children, but they are very rambunctious dogs. It is possible that a child could be hurt by their enthusiastic playing and loving. They are very powerful dogs. Having made that point, I would like to note that there are always exceptions to every rule. An example is Roxy, a 10-month-old Boxer. Her owners, Dawn and Gerry, have four little girls, and Roxy is exceptionally gentle and quiet around them. She seems to understand that they are more fragile than adults.

Another good family dog is the Newfoundland. This wonderful breed was awarded a gold medal in 1919 when a Newfoundland pulled some 20 shipwrecked people to shore. Since then, there have been numerous accounts of these brave dogs saving drowning people. They are extremely affectionate and loyal. But, they

Just because a breed is popular does not mean it will be right for your family. Most importantly, choose a dog that has a good temperament and an even disposition.

are very large and powerful dogs that need to be trained not to pull on the leash or knock people over.

Rufus, a 10-month-old Newfoundland, was enrolled immediately in training classes by his owners when the couple learned they were expecting a baby. They decided to enroll him in a group class so that he would be trained before the baby was born. Throughout the training, Rufus proved himself to be a very stubborn dog and talked back to his owners on several occasions. The group classes were wonderful for him because he learned to work for his owners and even grew to enjoy the attention. Initially, he was testing to see how serious they were about this training idea. Once he realized they were going to be in control, he responded beautifully. It is good that they worked through all of this before the baby came. Now, Rufus' true Newfoundland characteristics are showing, and he is a great family dog.

You also need to consider that the popularity of a dog may not mean the breed is a good choice for your family. An example of a breed that may not be right for you is the Rottweiler. In the latter 1980s and early 1990s, the breed became very popular. Due to overbreeding, the Rottweiler can be unstable and unpredictable. Although this breed has had a wonderful reputation with children, there have been a series of disturbing stories in the last few years about Rottweilers attacking small children and doing considerable damage. I know the problems of overbreeding or poor breeding all too well. On December 8, 1990, I had to put down my beloved Spenser, a two-year-old Rottweiler, because he had become increasingly aggressive and unpredictable. It was one of the most painful things I have ever had to do, but I had no choice. He was dangerous! I wouldn't want anyone else to ever have to go through this. Do not get a dog because he is the new "in" breed.

Rottweilers are only one example; in no way am I saying that the Rottweiler is an unacceptable companion for children. In truth, Rottweilers are fabulous dogs—great companions for children, adults, and other dogs if they have the right heritage. In fact, in *Dog's Best Friend,* Mark Derr downplays the importance of the pure breed because the smaller gene pool allows for a greater risk of genetic problems. Amen.

I do seriously caution you about the results of "backyard" breeding—that's when people decide their dogs are "pretty" and breed them without doing any research or making any attempt to study the dog's heritage, and the result of this lack of knowledge and experience can be disastrous.

If you think you would like a purebred dog, talk to breeders, vets, and trainers who have worked with the breed, but have no personal stake in a sale. If the dog is a mixture, try to determine what kind of mix he is. An example of an unfortunate mix would be a Gordon Setter/Samoyed mix. I knew one named Tikva. She was extremely loving, but stubborn and "dingy." The Gordon Setter in her ate alarm clocks and got locked in dark closets without the good sense to bark for help, and the Samoyed in her did not learn from the lessons—she would just do it all again.

However, all of this is not to say that once you have found the "breed for you," the test is over. Like people, all dogs are individuals. You may decide on the perfect breed only to find that the puppy you selected does not possess the overall characteristics of that breed. Again, ask your vet and a trainer to look at the puppy you are interested in. There are ways to test the puppy for behavioral characteristics. Regardless of whatever dog you choose, you will still have a major influence on what kind of dog your pup will grow up to be!

Last but not least, never get a pet to teach your child "responsibility." Pets are wonderful additions to the family and make great friends for your child, but ultimately, this living being is your responsibility. If the child fails this lesson, who suffers the most?

ALLERGIES

Just because you or someone in your house has allergies does not mean that you can never have a dog. There are several breeds you may consider. Talk to your vet. The Soft Coated Wheaten Terrier, for example, is perfect for allergy sufferers. The Basenji is another good "allergy-free" dog. They are very clean animals without a hint of odor. They are also excellent with children.

Depending on the severity of the allergy, you can work around some of the elements that may cause discomfort. It is not the hair, but the dander (scales) from the dog's skin and their saliva that cause allergic reactions. Brushing the dog and vacuuming the house daily will greatly reduce the amount of hair and dander floating around. There are also quite a few breeds that are noted for minimal hair loss—and the less fur the animal sheds, the less dander he sheds, too. Like the Soft Coated Wheaten Terrier, the hair loss in the following breeds is less harmful

Because he sheds less than other dogs, the Soft Coated Wheaten Terrier is one of several breeds that are perfect for people who suffer from allergies.

to the allergy sufferer because it stays within the coat: the Schnauzer (Miniature, Standard, or Giant), Bedlington Terrier, Kerry Blue Terrier, Portuguese Water Dog, Poodle, and Bearded Collie. These dogs require more brushing and grooming to avoid mats and tangles, but they are easier on the sinuses.

And what dogs do doctors recommend? Dr. Michael Kaliner, head of allergic diseases at the National Institutes of Health, says, "We'd recommend a dog like a terrier that does not shed or slobber. Boxers and Saint Bernards are my favorite dogs, but they are the worst for allergies."

For families with allergies, there is always the option that my family chose. My father and I were terribly allergic to animal fur (among other things) and took medication for years, allowing us the pleasures of owning Punkin and Tikva. After several years, I developed an immunity to animal allergies. If you have health problems, you should discuss the advisability of pet ownership with your doctor; you may not have to limit yourself to fish!

OTHER PETS IN THE HOUSE

If you already have other pets and are considering getting a dog, a puppy is definitely the easiest route. If there is another dog in the house or you are adopting two puppies, my recommendation would be to select dogs of the opposite sex, particularly if there is a male involved. Two or more females can live together, but there is often trouble with two males living in the same territory, even when they are neutered. That is not to say two males cannot live together. There are exceptions. Oliver and Barrymore were two male Dalmatians who were best buddies. They did "square off" from time to time, but they loved each other very much. Generally speaking, however, life is a lot less complicated if the pair is either two females or a male and a female.

Thinking about getting two puppies at the same time? There are pros and cons to this decision. It is like having twins—where one may be quiet and content to sleep on his rug, the other will run off and find a nice chair leg to chew on; one may be barking, while the other one watches quietly. Housetraining two puppies can be quite frustrating. However, many working owners feel that because they are not able to give a dog enough exercise time, it would be an advantage to have two puppies that will definitely wear each other out. Also, owners never have to worry about their pups being lonely when they are gone all day.

As long as they are properly introduced and carefully supervised, your dog should be able to get along with any other pets in the house.

The best arrangement, I believe, is to have one dog a year or two older than the puppy. This way, you can housetrain the pup and have the older dog show him "the ropes." Often, a pup will see the adult go outside to urinate and will follow his lead. The puppy will learn very quickly how hard he can or can't bite when he plays with the adult dog, or, in the case of my dog, the adult can show the puppy how to beg. (Well, even a trainer's dog has an occasional bad habit.) Additionally, the eventual loss of one dog can be minimized when you still have the other to hug and love.

GROOMING CONSIDERATIONS

Grooming your dog involves two things: time and money. This is especially true for breeds like the Lhaso Apso, Shih Tzu, Maltese, Poodle, Schnauzer, Cocker Spaniel, and Yorkshire Terrier. They need professional grooming about every eight weeks. The cost can be double for the larger breeds like the Giant Schnauzer,

Some breeds need more extensive grooming than others. The time you want to spend on grooming should be a consideration when choosing a breed.

Standard Poodle, and Old English Sheepdog. Even such breeds as the Chow Chow, Samoyed, Great Pyrenees, Newfoundland, Collie, Afghan, and Sheltie need an owner who is faithful to brushing his dog. A period without grooming can lead to terrible mats that must be cut out.

CLIMATE CONSIDERATIONS

It would seem to be obvious that the weather where you live would and should influence what breed you choose. However, many people are taken with a specific breed regardless of the heat or cold in their region. While attending college in Texas, I was amazed to see Great Pyrenees, Siberian Huskies, and Newfoundlands there. It would be 105 degrees outside, and someone would be walking a Husky. And, as I was writing this book, a friend from Louisiana called to get advice about getting a Komondor, a dog that has been used as a police dog in snowy regions. I talked my friend out of it for the dog's sake. He got a Bullmastiff instead.

If you have an outdoor dog, be sure that you provide the proper shelter. Consider what kind of breed the dog is and what he requires. For example, many people believe that the Doberman Pinscher makes an excellent outside guard dog. In truth, Dobies are very thin-skinned and cannot fight the cold elements very well. Watch the weather reports. When a cold snap or brutally hot day is reported, bring your dog inside. There is no other way to say this—if it is freezing outside, keeping your dog outside is cruel and inhumane. The same applies for intense

Different dogs have different activity levels and housing requirements. Some dogs, like this Bulldog, enjoy the comforts of home, while other breeds prefer to spend a lot of time outdoors.

heat. Since I mentioned Texas, I will use San Antonio as an example of the importance of appropriate shelter. San Antonio has a lot of electrical storms, which are always followed by reports of missing animals. When the storms suddenly come on, the animals outside become terrified and escape from their yards. They believe they are running for their lives, but, often, they are running to their deaths. Be sure that you provide proper, sturdy shelter for your pet.

CHOOSING THE RIGHT DOG FOR YOU

MALE OR FEMALE

Often, a new dog owner will buy a male dog believing that his protective instincts are stronger than a female's and that he will make a better watchdog. This is not true. In most cases, there is no real distinction between males and females in terms of which is the better watchdog. In some breeds, the male is usually more defensive and, in others, it is the female. As always, it also depends upon the individual dog.

Never allow a breeder to push a specific gender on you unless he or she truly knows your particular situation. For example, females are usually better for first-time dog owners. They are easier to train as pups, and they are generally smaller and easier to handle than males. The breeder may suggest that you start out with a female, particularly if the breed that interests you tends to be stubborn.

SPAYING OR NEUTERING

Although the issue of whether to spay or neuter a dog should not be a dilemma, it seems to be one for many people. I know people who seem to think that having the male dog neutered will make him less aggressive or "manly." Neither the male nor female becomes a less effective watchdog or companion when neutered or spayed. Neutering only changes the ability to sire or bear pups; it does not change your dog's personality. (Although it is true

Spaying or neutering your puppy helps to prevent your dog from contracting certain cancers of the reproductive system and improves his or her overall health.

that neutering an aggressive male dog may help his disposition.) Neutering may also prolong your dog's health and life by reducing the chances of prostate cancer and hernias; it may also reduce the defecation problems that unneutered dogs frequently experience later in life. Spaying, the procedure used for females, involves removing the ovaries and uterus, which decreases the risk of breast cancer and prevents ovarian tumors. However, the rumor you may have heard about female dogs being calmer after having puppies is not true.

Many of my clients have expressed guilt or distress over the idea of spaying or neutering their pet. Not too long ago I read an excellent response given by a vet to the question, "Aren't we taking away their rights to reproduce?" Dr. Bonnie Wilcox responded, "Rights? Her right to develop pyometra, milk fever, or uterine cancer, or to suffer the pain of multiple births or cesarean sections? His right to be frustrated, to develop testicular cancer, to wander off to his ladylove and be hit by a car or shot by an irate 'in-law?' Your right to deal with hostile phone calls, pay the vet bills, fight off males from your doorstep, mop the floor daily to cleanse the mess made by your female's season, and to worry?... Her right to have pups, only to have them taken away weeks later; his right to be a noncustodial father; and your right to care for puppies many hours each day?... Dogs only have the rights their

Breeding your dog is a big responsibility and should be done only by people who have the knowledge and facilities to care for the mother and all the resulting puppies.

owners give them, and we can give them the right to a peaceful, healthy nonparental life…Rights?"

Additionally, 15 million unwanted dogs and cats (the products of unneutered and unspayed parents) are killed each year! Even more suffer from homelessness. To reduce your pet's roaming (males following the scent of a female in heat), to prevent him from becoming hurt, stolen, or lost, and to reduce pet overpopulation and suffering, be a humane human and spay or neuter your pet. If you still need more convincing, statistics show that unneutered dogs account for as many as 80 percent of all dog bites!

When you adopt a dog from the animal shelter, the shelter will cover the cost of spaying or neutering, and you may be able to get a discount for the cost of shots and vaccinations. It is a great deal for everyone.

WHERE TO FIND YOUR DOG

Please do not buy a dog from a puppy-mill pet shop. Because dogs are pack animals, placing puppies side by side in individual cages, as these businesses do, has a severe impact on their behavioral and psychological conditioning. Puppies need socialization with other

To ensure against genetic diseases and to preserve the quality of their programs, responsible breeders will screen all of their dogs for health and temperament before breeding them.

puppies and people; the cage prevents such development. During the years I have trained, I have seen, as have most trainers, definite personality disorders in puppy-mill animals.

If you are set on getting a purebred puppy, go through a professional breeder. Do not buy from what trainers term a "backyard breeder"—that is, people who decide to have a litter of puppies because their dog is "pretty" or they believe that the animal has "good lines." In the 1970s, the Cocker Spaniel and the German Shepherd were very popular dogs, and, as would be expected, a lot of owners began to breed their Cockers or Shepherds. The results were disastrous. During the mid- to late-1980s, I began working with the offspring. I will never forget one of those offspring pups, Buster, a Cocker who kept attacking his owner. Every time his owner did something he did not like, Buster would charge him, gnashing his teeth.

Overbreeding always results in alterations of some of the characteristics that made the breed popular. The German Shepherd has been affected physically and is susceptible to hip dysplasia, which cripples the dog so severely that vets often recommend euthanasia. Dalmatians have become prone to deafness, and Dobermans and Boxers have become prone to cancer. Also, the disposition and reliability of Rottweilers has certainly changed. It seems that the worst thing that can happen to a breed is that it becomes popular. It may cost a bit more in time and money to select carefully and buy from a reputable breeder, but in the long run it will pay off.

When you talk to a breeder, ask for names of previous clients. If the breeder is willing to give references, call them. If the breeder will not or cannot, find another breeder. You may

Many dogs are given up to shelters because of behavior problems. Training is especially important in order to help your pound puppy acclimate to his new home.

often read or hear things like "the hips are guaranteed." This sounds like a good deal, but I have yet to meet an owner who, on discovering that his dog had bad hips, or any other problem, said, "Okay, back you go." Who is going to love, train, and live with a pup for two or three years and then, suddenly just return him to the breeder? No one. So, learning that the hips are guaranteed, or of any guarantee, doesn't really mean that much. Find out more about the dog's line. Talk to other clients of the breeder, and review the dogs' health records and pedigrees.

Animal Shelters

Sosi, my pound puppy, was about three months old when she came home with me. She was a safe bet—old enough to be thankful and young enough that I knew there could not be any personality traits ingrained in her yet. Of all my clients who adopted from the shelter, about 30 percent of them experienced problems with behavior. It is true, you do not always know why a dog is at the shelter. He may have been abandoned, or he may have been very destructive so the owner, unable to handle him, dumped him at the shelter. However, an equal number of my clients who got their dogs from a reputable breeder also experienced problems. That is why training is necessary. Many people want to get a pure breed, so they reject the animal shelter as a place to find a pet, but you can easily find all kinds of breeds there. Do not reject the idea of adopting a dog at the animal shelter. As many other pound-puppy owners will tell you, "My pound puppy is the best dog I have ever had!"

Pepsi was a Black Labrador and Cocker Spaniel mix (we think). She was over a year old when she was adopted. For the first few days, she was nervous in her newly adopted home. She was quiet, a little shy, and she left everything as it was. But after Pepsi began to feel more comfortable, she began tearing up everything in sight.

Her new owners brought Pepsi to me, and we began basic obedience training. We worked on leash training in the house so she would feel that the rules applied in the house as well as on the street. When they left her alone, they confined her to a smaller, puppy-proofed area. Finally, after she was feeling pretty relaxed with her training, we set her up. We would pretend to leave the house, but one person would remain hidden. When she began destructive behavior, that person would leap out of hiding and correct her behavior.

It required months of "surprise" set ups, constant training, and eventual expansion of her confined area—not to mention lots of patience—to correct the bad behavior that Pepsi had brought with her. But correct it, we did.

Joe, a beautiful Golden Retriever, was adopted when he was about two years old. I was suspicious at first. He was well groomed and well fed. Why would anyone let this gorgeous animal go unless he had real behavioral problems? As it turned out, he was absolutely perfect in the house, the backyard, the car—everywhere. He was housetrained and gentle and loving with children and other dogs. The moral of this story is when you adopt an adult dog, you usually cannot know the circumstances he comes from or how his personality has been affected. Sometimes you are lucky, like Joe's owner. Sometimes you're not. Like most owners, you and your dog have to work a bit. As a general rule, however, I would suggest adopting a puppy rather than an adult. If you get a puppy (any age under 10 months), it will be much easier to mold him to your own way of life.

You will often find females at the animal shelter that have just given birth to a large litter. Ideally, you want to get a puppy around eight to ten weeks old. No sooner! Puppies need to have time to socialize with their littermates and should not be weaned from their mothers too early. Many times, puppies who have been weaned too early are insecure and can have a variety of behavioral problems.

In addition to covering the cost of having the dog spayed/neutered and offering discounts with your local vet to have him vaccinated and examined, many shelters offer education and training classes. These classes can help you start off on the right foot. Behavior consultants are on staff to field questions and help you and your new pet adjust to each other. This is far more than any breeder in the paper or pet shop might offer. Finding a pet is a great responsibility and you should not go it alone. Utilize the many benefits of the Humane Society *and* save a little life!

When you adopt a dog from a shelter, you are not only gaining a companion, you are saving a life.

WHICH PUPPY TO PICK FROM THE LITTER

All litters contain puppies with different personality types. There are always the shy ones, the loners, and the aggressive ones. My family and I wish we had known that when we picked out our first puppy. One of the pups in the litter jumped over all the other ones and barreled her way over to me. I liked that. She chose me, I did not choose her. I felt it must be a sign that she liked us from the start. What I did not know then was that behavior of this type is often a sign of dominance and may indicate future problems. That was definitely true in this case. In fact, when all was said and done, I owed a great deal of thanks to Tikva. Tikva forced my family to learn about basic obedience and how to deal with behavioral problems.

Just as with the puppies that display signs of dominance or aggression with their siblings, it is also advisable to stay away from the shy, timid ones. The withdrawn puppies often snap at people through fear. A dog with this personality is particularly bad to have around children.

So what puppy should you pick? Try to find the puppy that plays well with the others—

The puppy you choose should be bright-eyed, healthy looking, interested in the world around him, and excited to be with you.

not the bully, not the meek one. Look to see if he responds to noises. If possible, try to see the puppies individually. You want the puppy who can pass a series of tests:

•*Attention Span:* Bring a toy with you. When you squeak the toy, watch to see if the puppy looks around. He should be naturally curious. Once you have his attention, continue to squeak the toy. See how long it can hold his attention—it should be for about 10 seconds. Keep squeaking. You can also clap your hands. Does the puppy come to you with his tail up? This is a good sign. Next, leave the room. If the puppy follows, this is another good sign.

•*Play Time:* Once you have held the pup's attention, toss him the toy. See how long he is able to play with the toy before losing interest. Avoid puppies that are timid or afraid of the toy.

•*Roll-Over:* You should be able to roll the puppy and scoop him into your arms and cradle him. The puppy should be so relaxed that you should be able to lift a paw and have it fall back down. If the puppy fights you, refusing to be held in such a submissive position, this tells you he is a very dominant puppy and may be difficult to handle. Ideally, you want a puppy that struggles for a few seconds, and then settles down, allowing you to hold him.

Whatever personality you choose, you will still have a major influence on what kind of dog your pup will grow up to be. What you do and say and how you do and say it will affect your pup's development.

Part Two:

HOW TO BEGIN

PUPPY HEAD-START

At the age of ten weeks, a puppy can begin some preliminary obedience training. This training merely lays a foundation for the more extensive basic obedience training that you will begin when your dog is older and able to handle the responsibility. When you begin training a puppy, it is important not to skip head-start and go on to basic obedience. After all, would you put a two-year-old child in first grade? No, because he wouldn't be able to keep up intellectually or emotionally. I've had many clients try to pay me to skip head-start training with their puppy and go right into basic obedience, but I wouldn't do it. These people didn't want to spend the time working their pups; they just wanted to drop them off at day care and then pick up little robots that were already trained for them. These people should not have dogs. However, if you already have an adult dog, you could skip ahead to basic obedience, although you may want to review this section.

WHO'S IN CHARGE?

Keep in mind that all dogs are pack animals and that in every pack there is a leader. One leader. Michelle's dogs don't know this. She has two Doberman Pinschers. They sleep in bed with her, under the covers. They suck—yes, suck—on her pillows (it's a long story) and lounge all over her furniture. In their minds, there is no leader. They are all one big, happy pack family. So, when Michelle expresses dismay that Kinder (it's always Kinder) doesn't listen to her or tears up her pillow, I remind her that Kinder really doesn't know any better. She has never been given clear guidelines. I can assure you of this: The alpha male (the lead wolf dog) doesn't share his pillow with any of his pack! It is important that you establish yourself as the pack leader from the very beginning of your relationship with your dog. Otherwise, because they are pack animals and instinctively must have a leader, your dog will eventually vie for the top dog position.

You must establish yourself as the leader. To gain this position, there are a variety of dominant gestures you can practice on your puppy. The techniques are subtle and gentle, but your puppy will get the message.

Scientists can actually discern the alpha male and the social hierarchy of a canine pack by its body language and by the way members of the pack greet each other. For example, when I come home after being away for a short while, my Lab-mix, Sosi, greets me with her ears pulled back, head flat, eyes squinted, and tail wagging (but held low). This is not the result of my beating her. (If truth be known, however, I did bonk her with a pillow three years ago, and she still remembers this as the time she nearly died.) Sosi greets me with true canine respect and affection. In turn, I greet her back as an alpha male would—I give her some pets, a kiss on the head, but then I move on. I don't spend 20 minutes dancing around the floor with her.

Michelle, on the other hand, receives a different reception from her Dobie, Kinder. As Michelle enters the house, Kinder affectionately says, "Yo, 'Chelle. What's happening?" Then, they proceed with their 20-minute, happy-dance ritual. Michelle is no different than most dog lovers. Her dogs truly love her. She truly loves them. But there is no clear guideline of who is who. Because I am going to be picking on Michelle throughout the book, I should clarify something now. One of her dogs, Kaiser, is very well-behaved and understands his role, and the two of them have a truly wonderful relationship. This is interesting because I trained Kaiser as a puppy.

Kinder, on the other hand, was never trained as a puppy. As a result, she is an insecure dog. She has learned a great deal from Kaiser, but because Michelle has not asserted herself as the "alpha male" with Kinder, Kinder still doesn't understand what all the rules are or what her role should be. For her, true canine respect is the missing key. And this respect is vital to laying the foundation for basic obedience, which is so important for your dog's confidence and reliability. It is also an important part of a healthy relationship that will involve trust, respect, and loyalty to you—the person who walks upright and has opposing

You can assume your role as pack leader by rolling your puppy over onto his back and rubbing his stomach. This puts him in a submissive position.

thumbs—as the leader!

Begin assuming your role as pack leader by teaching your puppy the following tricks and basic commands.

The Roll-Over

Practice rolling your puppy onto his back (a submissive gesture) until he will stay there and allow you to rub his stomach. His legs should be so relaxed that if you pick up a paw, it will fall back down. If his legs are stiff, he is resisting the roll - over.

Eye Contact

Check to make sure your puppy is not staring you down. If he holds steady eye contact, he is challenging your authority. Practice challenging his stare until he looks away. To get the best results possible in any form of training, it is imperative to build a rapport with your dog. You can begin building this relationship from the very first day you get your puppy.

During the day, or when you are able to be with the puppy for a good amount of time, tie the end of a six-foot lead to your belt loop or around your waist. This technique literally works like an umbilical cord. You will be amazed at how quickly your puppy will bond with you. Dogs that are raised with this method are highly receptive to the moods of their owners.

You may also tie the leash to something secure in an area where you can keep an eye on your pup and he may also see you, but be sure that he is wearing a flat collar and not a chain

Maintaining eye contact while training is very important. It helps to build a bond between you and your dog.

collar. You should never leave a chain collar on an unsupervised puppy or dog. The chain can catch on anything in the house and, in a panic, your dog could choke himself, or he might go over a piece of furniture and hang himself. In the yard, he can catch the chain on a fence, trying to go under or over it, and strangle himself. Never leave a chain collar on an unattended puppy or adult dog.

In addition to the safety issue, there are other reasons for using a flat collar on a puppy during training. He is too young to have a chain collar. Puppies that wear a chain collar can develop incredibly strong neck muscles. This will make training that much more difficult for both of you. (The neck is the second strongest muscle in the dog's body, the first being his jaws.) Also, you want the sound of the chain to be a surprise to him when you begin the training. For now, a flat collar will do nicely.

The Sit Command

To teach the sit command, start by facing your puppy. As you give him the command, say, "Sit," and gently push his bottom down so that he is in a sit position. Hold him there while you repeat, "Good sit." Offer him a treat and lots of praise. He will learn this trick in a week if you continue to practice it over and over every day. Be sure to say the command, "Sit," every time.

When you tell your puppy to sit, *do not* say his name. Only later in basic obedience training will you say his name with the commands given to heel and come. Because so many

To teach the sit command, face your puppy, give him the command, and gently push down until he is in the sit position. Hold him there while you praise him, and reward him with a treat.

When teaching the stay, keep your left hand up with the palm facing your dog. As his confidence builds, you can slowly start to put distance between you.

habits are formed now, take special precautions not to say the puppy's name with any other commands. If he does not sit on command, say, "No, sit," and push his bottom into a sitting position.

The Stay Command

Once your puppy has learned the sit, the stay command is an easy one to teach. When he sits, be sure to praise him and then tell him, "Stay." At first, hold him in place and repeat the command over and over. Be sure that your tone is firm but reassuring. Let him know that he is doing a great job of sitting there (even though you are holding him).

After a day or two, you may move your hand away from him just a little. Although you are not touching him, you are right there so that if he does move, you can instantly hold him again. Be sure he is still sitting. As his confidence builds, you can move farther and farther away. Repeat the command from time to time during the stay. When you are able to stand a distance away from him, keep your left hand up with the palm facing him. As a puppy, he probably won't be able to stay for very long; but as he grows and becomes more confident, his stays will get better and better. Praise him! "Good boy! Good stay! Good boy!" Note that I do not say his name, but I give him lots of reassurances.

A puppy's attention span is limited, so remember to keep initial training sessions short and pleasant, and always end with lots of praise.

PUPPY HEAD-START OBEDIENCE

By practicing obedience drills with your puppy, you will quickly establish yourself as the leader, and the puppy will learn to perform well as an adult with new training drills.

No extensive training should be done with your puppy until he reaches at least the age of four months. In some instances, puppies mature more slowly, and even four months of age may be too young to begin formal training. (My Shepherd mix, Nala, was abused as a pup and was not ready for real obedience training until she was nine months old.) Until then, be sure to use the following drills to lay the foundation for later training.

Before you begin obedience training, it is important to remind yourself of a few things. Keep in mind that your puppy is a baby. His attention span is very short; for example, when he sees a leaf blow across his path, it is fun and exciting to him. He will become easily distracted, so do not lose your temper. Use a soothing voice and show him what you want. If you want him to come to you, bend over and pat the front of your legs to invite him to you. Talk in a friendly voice. It is important that you are in a good and patient mood before you begin training, so that the experience will be pleasant and productive.

Recently, I had a client ask about the intelligence of her chocolate Labrador Retriever, named Moose. Her other dog is a Springer Spaniel, and she could not help but notice that her Springer was more receptive to training. I told her that Springers are very, very big people-pleasers. Pleasing their leaders is most important. They are intelligent and giving dogs. This is not to say the Lab is not, but the Lab puppy is a puppy's puppy. I can take a Springer and a Lab—same age—and put them through the same paces. Many times, the Springer will seem to be doing a little better. Is he smarter? Not at all. For the Lab puppy, and we'll use Moose as the example, he's doing a beautiful sit/stay when he sees…Gasp! A blowing leaf. He leaps to his feet, wildly excited to have seen this amazing thing: "A leaf! A leaf!" Snap. Correction. Verbal command. "Oh, right. Sorry. Where were we? Ah, yes, the stay. Ahem." Then, suddenly…Gasp! "Another leaf!" Understanding your pup's breed will help the training—not to mention your level of patience.

LEASH MANNERS

Begin by teaching your puppy appropriate leash manners right away. Always hold the leash in your right hand. (This will become important for the dog when you get to basic obedience, but it is important for you to begin developing good habits now.) Do not allow your dog to pull you. He may walk ahead of you on either side, but when he begins to pull, give him a slight tug backward and tell him, "Stay with me." Pat your left side and encourage

---

You should teach your puppy appropriate leash manners immediately. Hold the leash in your right hand and let it drop below your knee. As you walk, your leg will automatically correct the dog into the right position. Remember to praise him for a job well done.

him to remain there, holding the leash in your right hand. As often as he pulls, keep repeating this phrase. Be consistent, and eventually he will learn to watch you as he walks. He will not like being tugged or jerked and will watch you more carefully. Continue to tell him he is a good puppy, pat your left side and say, "Stay with me."

What you really want at this point is for your puppy to be comfortable with the leash and not to drag you around. It may not seem like a very big deal when he is so little, but as he pulls on his collar, his neck and chest muscles are developing and he will learn to pull harder and harder. That is why it is important that he wear a flat, nylon collar. Additionally, the sound of the chain correcting him may be distracting to him. Do not put a chain collar on him until he begins basic obedience.

The On-Leash Sit

While the puppy is on his leash, practice the sit command. Make sure he is on your left side while you are enforcing this command on leash. Gather up the leash in your right hand so that there is only a little bit of slack in it. With your left hand, gently push on your pup's bottom and give the command, "Sit." If he can sit without physical contact from you, that is great. Every time you stop, have him sit. Again, be patient. Eventually, he will learn that each time you stop walking, he is expected to sit automatically. This is an excellent start for basic obedience. And, remember, every pup moves at his own pace. Some dogs are very quick to pick up new lessons. Other dogs, for whatever reasons, are slower. For more immature breeds—like Newfoundlands, Boxers, and Labradors—a blowing leaf can be such a huge distraction it will be almost impossible for them to pick up on the sit command right away. It is not that they are dumb (quite the contrary), but there are many breeds that stay puppies longer than others. Be patient and be repetitive!

The On-Leash Stay

After you have made the puppy sit, use your left hand—palm facing the puppy—to make a sweeping gesture from right to left in front of his eyes as you tell him, "Stay." Stand very close to him so that you can catch him right away when he stands. Puppies tend to think that as soon as you drop your hand they can pop up. Therefore, while your puppy is learning to stay, you may take your left hand and hold the leash above his head, so that he feels a slight pressure and knows that he should still stay. Do not pull on the leash—leave some slack. Holding the leash between your thumb and forefinger, turn your hand upward.

When teaching the on-leash stay, hold the leash slack between your thumb and your forefinger and use the hand signal in conjunction with the verbal command.

If the puppy tries to move out of the sit position, lift up the leash, telling him, "No." This will force the puppy to remain in a stationary position. As you lean over him, he will automatically drop into a sit. Remember, because he is a puppy, everything will be a distraction to him, and he will quickly forget that he is supposed to be in a sit/stay position. Do not allow yourself to get frustrated by this. As you practice the commands with him, and as he gets older, you will see great improvements.

TRICKS

Teaching your puppy a variety of tricks enables him to learn more easily, and it trains him to work for praise. As a result, later training will come more quickly and easily. As long as your pup is happy, he can be taught tricks. It is up to you to be patient, offer lots of praise, and see that he is enjoying himself. Check to see that his tail is wagging, that he is alert, and that he appears to love the attention. He will not learn any tricks right away because he is a baby, but in time he will master them. Patience! Remember, you cannot reason with him as you can with a person, so you must be ready to praise him the minute he does what you are asking.

Getting your puppy to give you a kiss is easy; just give the command every time he kisses you and praise him afterward.

Give Me a Kiss

Every time your puppy kisses you or the two of you are face to face, say, "Give me a kiss." Puppies love to kiss, so this will not be a problem. The minute he kisses you, praise him, hug him, and pet him. Every time he is going to kiss you, give the command. It may seem silly, but he will learn the phrase and will oblige on command later. It will also teach him to kiss only on command, if you don't like constant canine kisses.

Find the Ball

This trick is particularly good for retrievers, but all dogs love it. Get a couple of tennis balls. Put your pup in a sit position, tell him to stay, and show him the ball. Place the ball several feet in front of him where he can easily see it. Be very enthusiastic and tell him to "find the ball." When he goes to the ball, praise him highly. Play with him and the ball a little. Try it again. As he gets used to the terminology, place the ball farther and farther away.

Once he has mastered this part of the trick, have someone stay with him to see that he still sits and stays. Go out of sight to place the ball. Do not hide it yet. Again, say, "Find the

Teaching your puppy a variety of tricks enables him to learn more easily and makes training sessions more fun. This German Shepherd happily retrieves the ball.

ball." Most likely, he will just follow the sound of your voice. When he sees you, repeat the command over and over until he spots the ball and picks it up. Praise him.

As soon as he masters this phase, begin to hide the ball. Do not make the hiding places too difficult. Point out the ball if you must. Do not let him get too frustrated. Spend several days in each new area where you hide the ball. Eventually, he will learn to sniff out the ball for himself. Remember to praise him each time he does.

This is a helpful trick because the pup has to really concentrate on staying while you hide the ball, and he must think to find it. It is a great exercise.

Hide-and-Seek

In the canine world of ball-chasers, I've had some duds. My dog, Tasha, is far too much of a snob to be bothered with chasing or seeking out a ball. And then there's Sosi. I threw a Frisbee™ to her once, and it curved around and bopped her on the head. Now she runs from things I throw.

If you have a ball-chasing snob or nitwit, the hide-and-seek game can be very rewarding. Again, it is a great exercise because it teaches your dog to sniff you out and become very

When your dog is in the sit position, give him whatever command you choose, lift his paw, and shake it. Soon your dog will give you his paw on his own.

aware of your movements and of noises in his environment.

My husband and I tell Tasha or Sosi to sit and stay. Repeating the command, "Stay," we slowly leave the room and hide. At first, we started out easy, hiding behind a door right around the corner. As Tasha and Sosi's stays and searching skills developed, we moved farther and farther away, hiding in closets, under beds, in the shower, etc. Oh, the joy when they found us! It turns out that Tasha, Miss Snob herself, loves this game, and even at 12 years of age, she is always ready for a good game of hide-and-seek.

Shake Hands

Again, you can use whatever expression you like when teaching this command. Sosi responds to "How do you do." Place your puppy in a sit position. Facing him, stretch out your right hand and give him the command, "How do you do." Of course, he will not know the command, so pick up his right paw and shake it. "Good boy! Good 'How do you do!'" Repeat this over and over. Some trainers will lightly rap on the paw they want to shake. When they do this, the pup will lift that paw, and the trainer then shakes it. Either method is acceptable.

Repeat this trick, like every other one, until your puppy gains confidence. Treats may help him to be more motivated. Again, the minute he raises his paw on his own, praise him highly. Always be sure that your pup is seated before you try the trick. And remember, it is okay if he is a "lefty" and will only raise his left paw, as Kinder does. If this is the case, put

The "high five" is an easy command to teach, especially if your puppy uses his paws a lot. Here, Abigale shows how it's done.

out your left hand to take his left paw, so that you don't confuse or frustrate him.

High Five

The "high five" is a very easy trick for pups that paw a lot. When Spenser was a pup, every time I had him sit, he would paw at me. I would catch my hand under his paw in a high five motion and repeat the phrase. In no time, he was "high five-ing" on command. Just like the shake command, repeat this command several times and offer lots of praise and rewards.

Bang! Bang!

Once your puppy has learned the down command, you can teach him to fall down when you cock your finger and shoot him. Start slowly by cocking your finger like a gun and telling him, "Down." (Of course, he should already know the down command.) After several down commands in a row, using the same tone of voice tell him, "Bang!" Repeat. If he knows the down command well enough, it will only take a few sessions of "shooting" before he will go down on a bang command.

As your trigger finger and his down become more proficient, you can get fancier and shoot him several times until he has learned to drop his head to the floor on the third bang.

INTRODUCTION TO BASIC OBEDIENCE TRAINING

When your puppy is at least four months old, he will be ready to begin basic obedience training. Once you begin a training program, you won't believe how much it means to your dog to train with you. Training time is quality time that will bond the two of you even closer, and you will be able to establish some rules that will make your lives easier and happier. Examples of trainer/dog bonding are Ace (a young Labrador), Lacy (a Boxer), and their respective owners—all from one of my group classes. We would meet every Monday evening and work for about an hour. I had only worked Ace and Lacy three or four times, but as soon as they saw me, they became very excited, leaping around me as though I were a long-lost friend. Their owners were amazed at how much their dogs loved me. In truth, Ace and Lacy knew when they saw me that they were going to work, and they loved it. They were thrilled to see me because they knew this was their "special time."

Keep in mind that you may not succeed with training at first. Patience is the key to training. "Mistakes do not equal failure"—my mother told me that once, and it has always stuck with me. I've made a lot of mistakes, but the list of successfully graduated pups is long. Dogs are very forgiving about our mistakes. I tell my clients again and again that every now and then they will have a terrible workout with their canine partners, but if they stick with it, the next workout will be better. As you move into the sometimes monotonous,

When working with your dog, a six-foot cotton web or nylon leash is best, because they are lightweight and comfortable.

sometimes frustrating part of training, always remember to be patient, to keep your temper, and to practice, practice, practice. The more you work your pup, the better he will be. All too often, we expect animals to make all the changes for us, but training is a partnership. If your dog doesn't understand something, show him what you want through body language, not shouting. Training should be a positive experience for both of you.

NECESSARY EQUIPMENT

Basic obedience is just that, learning the basics: heel, sit, down, stay, and recall. By incorporating these skills in your dog's life, he will be better behaved in every aspect. However, there are several tools and terms you must get familiar with before you begin training.

Leashes

You'll need a six-foot cotton web or nylon lead (leash). Cotton or nylon leads are lightweight so that they are comfortable for both you and your puppy. Do not use chain leashes, because their noise and weight are distracting to the pup in the beginning of training. Additionally, for some corrections, you could easily hurt your own hand. Stay away from chains.

Do not use leather leads if you can help it. I have seen leather snap. Also, the thicker leather materials are difficult for the trainer to handle. Kinder, the Doberman, recently was sporting a new pink, round (tubal) leash. While she looks pretty cute with her neon-pink leash, it is very difficult to double up in the trainer's hand. For "looking-cute" walks, this leash is fine. For working, the cotton web leashes are easier to handle; they fold easily in your

A young puppy should wear a flat buckle collar during his daily routine; you can switch to the chain collar when you are training.

hand and are quite strong.

Again, bad habits are formed during this time by both canine and human. While it may seem cute to let Fido play tug-of-war with his leash, trust me, it's not. As Fido gets older, he may try chewing on the lead, or he may think he can begin a game of tug while training—playing tug with a 125-pound dog is not fun. Discourage your pup from mouthing the lead.

Training Collars

Before you buy a training chain collar or "choke" chain (I really don't like that name), be sure to measure your dog's neck and get a chain several inches larger than that measurement. Also, for large breeds like the American Staffordshire Terrier, Rottweiler, Mastiff, and even some Retrievers, consider the size of the dog's head. Many times the chain collar won't fit over his head because it is so large and box-shaped. Do not buy poor-quality chains. I have often seen a chain snap when a trainer gave a correction. Suddenly, there you are and you have no hold on the dog at all. I have found that chains made in Germany and the US are very durable.

To put a collar on correctly, make a "P" shape, with the "P" facing you. Facing your pup, place the collar over his head. Because the dog is to be trained on your left side, the "P" ensures that the collar is most effective. When you administer a correction, the collar will release quickly because of the angle at which it rests on the dog's neck. If you have the chain on backward, it won't release enough to let you give effective corrections.

For dogs with heavy coats, you may need to stick your fingers between the neck and

To put a chain collar on correctly, make the letter "P" shape, and facing your dog, slip it over her head.

TEACHING BASIC OBEDIENCE • TRAIN THE OWNER, TRAIN THE DOG

You should hold the leash with your right hand. With your right thumb in the handle, pick up the slack so that your hand rests comfortably in front of you. Leave your left hand free to pat your side, praise your dog, and give hand signals.

collar periodically to free the collar of hair.

HOW TO HOLD THE LEASH

This is important! When you begin to train, the dog will learn to train on your left side. Because of this, all signals should be administered with the left hand, so you need to keep your left hand free. It stands to reason, then, that your right hand should hold the leash. While you walk, use your left hand to pat your side, which will guide your pup and let him know where you want him to be. Simple, right? This, however, is the hardest part of training for the human part of the duo. It seems natural that, because your dog is at your left side, your left hand should guide the lead. For one thing, it feels easier. Nevertheless, it is more distracting to the pup and, in the long run, more cumbersome for you. So, try to tell yourself again and again to keep that left hand off the leash. I promise, I will remind you often. (Forgive me, but I know how many times you are going to forget.)

So, then, how do you hold the leash? With your right thumb in the handle loop of the leash, close your hand around the handle. Practice this standing by yourself. Pretend that the leash is on your pup.

The leash will cross in front of your legs. This is why the "P" shape of the collar is important. The angle of the correction is perfectly aligned with the angle of the lead and the collar. Once you begin the training, I will often tell you to "gather up" the lead. By this, I mean that you need to use the left hand to pick up the slack in the leash to give a proper correction. Once you have done this, you will immediately drop your left hand from the

When giving a correction, throw both hands together and correct straight out to the side. Make the correction quickly and make it hard enough to catch the attention of your dog.

lead. If you can, tell a training partner to remind you frequently about your left hand.

When your left hand is on the lead, it becomes very natural for you to allow your pup to get farther and farther ahead. This is because you unconsciously take up the slack in the lead, and your pup will begin to strain against his collar, forging ahead, with you trying to hold him back. When he feels the steady pressure of his collar against his neck, he is no longer concentrating on heeling. You are right back where you started. Using your left hand allows a vicious cycle to develop.

HOW TO GIVE A PROPER CORRECTION

You have learned how to put the collar on properly and how to handle the lead, but all of this is meaningless unless you can give good, effective corrections. There are several different ways to correct depending on the size of your pup. But first, here are some general rules.

Always give a verbal correction with the physical one. As you and your dog progress, you may give verbal commands only, but never give just a physical correction. Also, when you correct, do not correct in an upward motion. An upward correction uses a lot of energy on your part, and it has no real impact on the pup. Be sure to correct using a motion that is straight out from the dog's neckline. In most cases, this means you are going to have to bend over slightly. You want the correction to be as streamlined as possible. It is important that the correction be made with a quick, snapping motion.

Do not be afraid to correct smaller dogs. If you correct your dog firmly and consistently, he will soon know what is expected of him.

Correcting Smaller Dogs

You need not be afraid to correct the smaller breeds. "But he's so small," two of my clients would say as Dusty, their four-year-old Dachshund, refused to sit. He knew that he did not have to sit because—here's the clincher—who was going to make him? Dusty would grin. In truth, little dogs are pretty tough. I created hours of entertainment outside business offices when I trained small dogs like Jack Russell Terriers. Once those little guys locked their legs and refused to go down, it was a full-out wrestling match. I always won, but it wasn't pretty. The terriers, in particular, are a pretty tough bunch. But then, any dog who would run face first into a badger or rat den and drag out a rodent his own size has got to be pretty tough. See, we forget about those tiny details when we say, "Oh, but he's so small." Obviously, you are not going to correct a Cocker Spaniel in the same way you would a Mastiff, but he still needs to be corrected firmly and properly.

I have a second favorite dog training book called, *The Monks of New Sketes: How To Be Your Dog's Best Friend.* These monk/dog trainers say that you know that you have corrected the dog sufficiently when you hear a slight yelp. Actually, I do not think you should go for a yelp, but you should get a response. If you tell your dog to sit and he stares at you after a week of training, you are not correcting him—you're tickling him. Correct him hard enough to get an *immediate* response. Snap! "Ohhhh! You want me to sit..." Often, with a smaller breed, it helps if you bend lower to the ground and lower your arm so that it is even with the dog's neck. He will feel the correction more.

No matter what their size, all dogs retain some of their original instincts and will need proper obedience training in order to become enjoyable companions.

The truth is that many of the smaller breeds of dog can be very stubborn. Because your pup was so small for months and months, it was probably easier for you to carry him around. Now, you suddenly want him to not only walk, but to listen to your commands. One of you is in for a rude awakening. Make it your dog. Keep in mind that basic obedience carries over into other aspects of his life and yours.

Speaking of other aspects of your dog's life…Can you imagine how humiliating and frustrating it must be to train a Maltese that is wearing little sweatpants and a sweatshirt with a hood and drawstrings? Or a toy Poodle wearing a mink coat? No, I am not kidding. Yeah, well, try teaching basic obedience to ten pounds of fluff dressed in the latest doggie workout wear, or a mink worth more than your car. Now, I ask you—do you really think that Little Ricky the Maltese or Doodle the Poodle wanted to be in those outfits? Okay, maybe Doodle liked her mink, but Little Ricky had the worst of both worlds. First, he truly believed he was a little prince and shouldn't be made to do anything he didn't want to do. And second, he was the laughing stock of the dog school. The pearl gray-colored sweatsuit with pink trim did nothing for his image. (Not to mention that we had to take his pants off every time he needed to do his business.) The point is this: No matter what the size, your puppy is still that—a puppy, a canine, a dog, a pooch, a four-legged little fur ball—not a human!

Correcting Larger Dogs

For most people, medium-sized dogs are the easiest to handle. They are just at the right height, so you only have to lean over slightly, and they are large enough that most owners feel comfortable giving corrections. This makes training go a lot faster. Remember the monks' advice—enough of a correction to get a response.

For the larger dogs, like Mastiffs, Great Danes, or Old English Sheepdogs, the same rule applies: The correction should be given at a level even with the dog's neck. Pull straight across, and snap the lead. Remember not to drag it—snap it. Because you are dealing with such a large animal, you are allowed an exception to the "no-left-hand" rule for corrections. I have found that women, in particular, have a difficult time making effective corrections with large dogs. Therefore, with large dogs, you may put both of your hands together, fist against fist, and correct in an outward motion. As always, a verbal correction should go with the physical one.

If you follow the natural line of the collar on the dog's neck, you will see that to give an effective correction, you should correct straight out to the right. I step out slightly to the right so that I can put a little weight behind the correction. If I were to correct straight up, which is what you may be inclined to do, the correction would be minimal; in fact, the dog might not feel it at all.

If you get into the habit of giving bad corrections, I guarantee your pup will start ignoring you. *Make sure each correction is effective.* If you are having a problem giving an effective correction, high-collar your dog. By this, I mean gather up the slack in the lead and, with your left hand raise the chain collar so that it is just behind his ears. This part of the neck is more sensitive, and a correction like this will definitely get his attention. Once he has been high-collared, however, keep the chain high behind his ears. This means there is constant pressure there to keep the collar from slipping down and keep his attention. He will be instinctively wary of the collar being so high. Your dog knows he is more vulnerable. Only a few good corrections need to be given using the high-collar position. Then, you should be able to resume the normal training methods and let the collar relax around his neck. The purpose of the high-collar position is to tell your dog to quit clowning around and pay attention—you are serious.

I suggest using this collar position with larger dogs when another dog passes by or when you are being ignored—*but be careful.* If you raise the collar too quickly (and with too much slack), your dog may be able to jerk his head out of the collar, which is the last thing you want. He might bolt and could get himself seriously injured or worse. Please, be careful.

Correcting larger or aggressive dogs may be more difficult. With the leash, bring the dog's collar up high behind his ears and give a firm and quick correction.

Raise the collar slowly and have your hand ready to tighten the slack the moment he begins to wiggle his head. And, if you are a Doberman owner, be prepared for the fastest neck-jerking in the West! These dogs can really move quickly.

Corrections or attempts to give proper corrections can be very frustrating. Before you lose your temper, consider two things: the breed/size of your dog, and your own physical condition. Larger dogs, naturally, are harder to correct. And what about the dog's age? How old is he? Before you began training, did he used to drag you everywhere? Yes? Then, his neck muscles are already very well-developed and tightness around his throat will not bother him too much. If he is older, this is a habit for him. What is his breed? Is he a sled dog? Sled dogs are born to pull. Their necks are as solid as rocks. Is the breed stubborn by nature? Think about these things before you begin and know what you are up against. Training can still be effective, but you will be required to have more patience and give good, firm corrections.

Who is Correcting?

And what about you? Are you a small person? Do you have some sort of disability that must be worked around? A client of mine, Mr. S., trained from his wheelchair. The first step to successful training with Mr. S. and Max, his Golden Retriever, was that Mr. S. used strong corrections from the very start. His booming voice barking out verbal corrections was also a must! It was very difficult to administer corrections when the chair was moving, so we had to give Max the impression from the start that he needed to pay attention.

If you have special needs or physical restrictions, it is important to have a partner who can help you in the initial stages of training.

If you are in a wheelchair, it is important that you have a non-wheelchair-bound partner, at least initially. For safety reasons, it is good to have a partner (or trainer) who can help lay the foundation for heeling. Mr. S. lent me his racing wheelchair to train Max. While I sat in the chair, another trainer pushed the chair. We did this so that, when I needed to correct Max for forging ahead, I could correct immediately. Had I been alone, by the time I had stopped wheeling the chair and picked up the slack to correct Max, he would have hopped back to where he was supposed to be. With the other trainer pushing the chair, I was able to correct Max as soon as he made mistakes.

Also, as someone who went flying down King Street in midday traffic in a wheelchair because Max spotted a cat, I am very sensitive to the safety issue. Once we hit high speed, it was impossible for me to effectively correct him. He was only in the beginning stages of training and had not yet learned to respond to the voice and mild corrections. He had not yet learned to resist the temptation of a cat. (And by the way, when they say "racing" wheelchair, they ain't lyin'!) If you have physical limitations, recruit someone else to do the initial training, but be there for every part of the training. If you are not present, the dog will decide he has to listen to the "trainer," but not to you. Be active in the training process. As you will see, there is so much that you can do in the home to enhance your dog's training.

Another one of my clients, Mr. P., had Parkinson's disease. Because of this, his physical and verbal corrections were weak. His two-year-old Cocker, Pooh, was anything but. It was imperative that Mr. P. did a lot of at-home training. We worked on long stays while the pup

When training your dog, you must find the way that works best for you. Physical praise and affection, coupled with effective corrections, are a critical part of successful training.

wore a leash in the house. Although the Cocker was always active on walks, the long down/stays helped remind him he must listen to Mr. P. A mutual respect developed between them. Mr. P. knew that he could never give Pooh the kind of corrections I could. Pooh knew it, too. So, for Mr. P, the very best training he could do with Pooh were long down/stays in the house and in the front yard. Mrs. P. was more active in the physical aspect of the training.

For smaller people, particularly women, the two-handed correction is very effective. As frustrating as it is, dogs tend to be real chauvinists. Whenever I train with a couple or a family, in almost every case, the dog listens to the man but not the other members of the family (even if the woman is the disciplinarian). The tone of a man's voice is much more commanding, and generally speaking, men administer much more forceful corrections. Also, many women do not have the upper-body strength necessary to give powerful corrections.

However, women are generally more successful than men in training because of the enthusiasm in their voices and their high level of praise and physical affection. In Mark Derr's book, *Dog's Best Friend,* he notes that in the world of the working-class dog, training has been historically abusive or harsh. It was not until the late arrival of female trainers that training styles changed. When women began to win in open competition, men began to switch their styles of training to more gentle techniques. Men must learn to use more physical praise and affection, and women must learn to use their hips to give solid, firm corrections.

Effective, consistent corrections are a critical part of successful training.

VERBAL PRAISE AND COMMANDS

Your voice is your most effective training tool. Your tone says everything. From the very start, your pup will learn to respond to your voice. High-pitched voices, squeals, and laughter mean praise to him. Deep tones, bellowing, and even a stern monotone voice can be very threatening or sound dangerous. I have found that when a dog is being stubborn about a particular command during training, it is the woman who has a more difficult time correcting. The deeper tones of a man's voice are generally threatening enough that the dog will obey him first. However, praise comes more easily for women, and dogs are very responsive to their tones. I am continuously telling my male clients to use more animation for praise and my female clients to lower their voices for their commands. This advice will work for you, too.

As you give verbal commands, watch your dog's body language to be sure your delivery is producing the effect you want. Watch your pup's tail and feet. When you begin the training and while you are heeling him, look back at his tail. Is it tucked between his legs? This means he is nervous or frightened. Perhaps he thinks he is being punished. If it is a curly tail, is it dropped? If you have a Doberman or another breed with little or no tail, watch his hindquarters. Are they tucked? Is his back arched? Ears pulled back? You need to talk to him and reassure him. Use a higher tone of voice. Praise him and reach down with your left (free) hand and stroke his ear occasionally. This will relax him and let him know that the training is a positive thing. Watch his feet. When you see that he is almost prancing next to you, this is a sure sign of success. When his feet are happy, he is happy, too.

The most important thing to remember is to keep your voice very upbeat while you are training—upbeat, but not too excited. If your voice is too excited or too high, your pup will lose all control and begin bounding around happily, and then you've lost control. Training should be a positive experience for both of you.

BASIC OBEDIENCE

TRAINING: PHASE ONE

O kay, we're ready to begin. You now have the collar on your dog in the proper "P"-shape position, and you know how to give a proper correction. The first step is to familiarize yourself and the pup with the collar and the lead. Sure, you have been on walks together, but now you are going to apply some rules.

First and foremost, your dog is to remain on your left side at all times. Do not allow him to go between your legs, to the right of you, or in front of you. Certainly, he will not understand what you want at first. It is important that you be very patient. Try to find an unpopulated area to practice in, preferably a parking lot. Parks and fields are full of interesting distractions. Eventually, you want to be able to work around these distractions, but for now, it will be easier on both of you if you avoid the various smells, sights, and noises.

There are only two times during training that you should say your pup's name. The first is when you begin the heel command. Each and every time you start to heel (starting with the dog in a sitting position), say, "Puppy, heel" (preferably using your pup's name, so you don't confuse him). Say it with enthusiasm. He should not think of training as something to dread. Remember, your tone of voice is everything. Let me clarify: When your pup is in a sit position, and you begin the heel, you always say his name and the command, "Fido,

As you progress with teaching your dog the heel command, you should stop periodically and have her perform a sit. You may want to use your left hand or your right foot to push the dog's bottom down. Always remind your pup of the command by telling her, "Sit! Good girl!"

heel." If you make a correction during the heel (for example, if your pup pulls ahead of you and you correct him back), you simply say, "No, heel."

Your objective during your initial working sessions is to have your pup realize what you want. Every time he crosses over to your right side, gently tell him, "No, heel," and pat your left side. Pull him over to your left side and continue to walk. I know it can be very frustrating, but he will eventually get it. Watch out for those little dogs. When they dart over to the right, they can really trip you up. Personally, I think Dachshunds do it on purpose!

If you have a pup that lunges every time he forges ahead, stop and let him hit the end of the lead. This way, he is correcting himself—the best form of correction. He will turn and look at you to see why you have stopped. Tell him "No, heel" and pat your left side. When you continue to walk again, he will rush forward, and you should stop and hold the leash firmly and, again, let him hit the end of the lead. Repeat the command. After about the fifth or sixth time, he will become suspicious of you and will learn to watch you more carefully. When he sees you stop, he will turn to face you. Immediately praise him and pat your left side, repeating the command, "Heel." Stick with it, and you will see how easily he responds.

Each time you set out to walk again, use the command "Fido, heel." Do not bellow this command. Sound pleasant, as if you are anticipating a good time. Remember that if the pup thinks of this as a fun exercise, he will be eager to learn. You must be persistent and consistent, or he will fight you. The more stubborn breeds will resist, but will also often understand more quickly what you want. The first thought in their stubborn minds is: "No way am I going to walk on just one side. We've been doing just fine the way we have been." Believe me, I have seen that look many times. Do not give up or give in. You can and will win.

Periodically, stop and have your pup perform a sit. That is, when you come to a stop, gently push your dog's bottom down as you give the command, "Sit." To do this, as you are preparing to come to a stop, begin to reel in the leash so that you have more control over your dog. Each time he sits, remember to praise him. Be sure that you do not say his name now, just the command. (You will use his name when you begin to heel again, and when you are calling him out of the sit. Remember that you will use his name only with the heel and recall commands, so that he always associates hearing his name with coming to or coming with you.)

One of the biggest obstacles for my clients to overcome when they are training is the awareness of other people. While my people may work really well with their pups when they are alone, they suddenly become shy when other people are around, not correcting

To perform a sit while heeling, stop, gather the lead in your right hand, and gently push down on your dog's bottom. Notice the trainer is leaning over the dog in a dominant position and that her right hand is raised slightly so she can give an immediate correction if he breaks position.

something that needs correcting because they don't want to bring attention to themselves. Overcome this shyness as quickly as possible. I always tell clients to just stare down at the pup. You don't even have to look at whoever is passing by. Just concentrate on your puppy. Trust me, as someone who had to train a Poodle wearing a mink, you learn to block out everything but your dog. Inevitably, people will stop to watch you—they may be interested in training, they may just be bored, or they may even think you are mistreating your pup. I once was working with a Siberian Husky named Igor. When Igor lunged at me and tried to take my face off, I corrected him hard, and put him in an alpha roll over. This happened just as someone came around the corner and threatened to report me to the ASPCA. Murphy's law. (This problem will be discussed later in the section on aggressive dogs). Don't worry about anyone else. Just concentrate on training your pup!

Never lose your temper with your dog. I will say this over and over again because it is perhaps the single biggest thing that ruins a workout. Pups will be pups. They love to tease and push you as far as they can. Losing your temper only ruins the lesson, turning everything into a game (because getting you angry constitutes play for some rascals). At that point, the lesson is over, and you have lost the round.

Use a command like "Okay" to indicate that your dog has performed well and that the session is over. Most dogs will eventually respond with great pride and excitement.

Also, never let your dog quit during the training session—you are the one who should say when the workout is finished, not your pup. After you are done, use a word that indicates to him that training is over and be consistent with that word. I use the command, "Okay." Woe to those who stand in the way after I tell my dog, Tasha, "Okay"; there is great Doberman excitement.

YOUR FIRST TRAINING SESSION

All right, go to it. Yes, right now. Put the book down and go get your puppy and leash. You need to practice for about 15 minutes. Both of you will be pooped when you return. (Before each of your sessions, refer to the sample workout guide shown later in the book to monitor your progress.)

I cannot say enough how important it is that you do not lose your patience or temper. Particularly if you have a stubborn dog or a playful puppy—you will be tested. While I trained Lacy, the Boxer, he drove me mad. He was an especially playful puppy. He did well with his lessons, but he was so young and so large. While we worked, he would untie my shoelaces to play tug-of-war, causing me to nearly fall on top of him. When I pushed him away, he wildly grabbed my arm, mouthing and slobbering on me. (For those who don't know, Boxer slobber can be quite excessive.) When he was in a sit and I began teaching him the down command, he would grab my hair, slobber all over my head, happily grab at my arms, and playfully bite my shirt.

Always keep your right hand on the leash; the use of the left hand causes a vicious cycle. Once the owner begins to pull back on the lead with the left hand, the dog feels the tugging sensation and instantly begins to forge ahead. Also, it allows for no eye contact or communication between the dog and owner.

It was all a test. I never lost my patience. I never showed anger. How could I when everyone was laughing? I would tell him, "No," correct him, and start the command over again. I would not play or get angry; I would simply correct him (verbally and physically), and repeat the command. I did this over and over again until he saw that testing me was not going to be any fun. Then, he would sigh heavily and do what was asked of him.

In the weeks that followed, Lacy still tried to play during classes. I stopped wearing shoes with laces. The first time I wore sandals, he licked and nibbled my toes. Not only did that trip us up, but the slimy slobber between my toes became so distracting I couldn't take it anymore. I learned to wear my hair tucked up in a baseball cap and wear close-toed, non-laced shoes until we worked through his shoe and hair fetish.

The key is: *Do not give up!* Keep after it. When your pup sees that you are determined to do this without losing your cool, he will oblige. And, remember, keep that left hand off the lead.

Welcome back. Now that you've practiced, you should begin to feel a little better with the leash. Remember, the left hand is the free hand; the right hand holds the leash. You will need to be reminded of this frequently. In fact, go get a piece of paper and write *"No left hand"* on it and tape it to your refrigerator. Not only will you see it constantly, but other people in the house can remind you of it as well.

When giving the heel command, step off with your left foot and pat your side to encourage your dog to stay with you.

Working on Heeling

Now that you've had your first session with your friend, it's time to get down to the business of heeling. When you begin your next lesson, immediately have your pup sit. From the sit position, tell him "Fido, heel," and begin walking. When your pup's chest is more than four to five inches in front of or behind your shin and knees, he must be corrected back into the proper position at your side. Make a right turn (because it forces your dog to pay attention and follow) and correct simultaneously, saying, "No, heel." Pat your left hip and talk to your pup. He should run up to your side. Once he is there, tell him, "Good boy" (or "girl" if that is appropriate). Most likely, not more than a second later, he will be ahead of you or behind you again. Repeat the correction. If he is dragging behind you, use a lot of animation in your voice and really praise your pup to encourage him to stay up there with you.

If your pup is heeling correctly, both rings of his chain collar should be touching. This indicates that he is staying close to you and not pulling. If the chain is taut against his neck, he is not heeling. You are simply holding him back and really building up his neck muscles (not to mention your biceps). It is virtually impossible to give an effective correction when the chain is taut because you can't get any snap. You should keep the collar loose and, when your pup needs correcting—snap—pop the correction quickly. Immediately release. The chain should be comfortable again.

If the collar is taut, there is a trick you can use to regain control. When I jog with Kinder, my sister's Dobe, she likes to sneak forward. When she does this, I give a little tug on the lead that naturally pulls her back and gives me more lead to play with. Then, when she pulls ahead again, I administer a heavy correction with a "No, heel." That gets her attention. You will be rewarded if you are persistent and consistent. When I jog with Sosi, she doesn't even wear a lead. She runs right beside me the whole way.

While you are training your pup to heel, you should walk in an oval pattern using right turns. It is not uncommon to get dizzy while training beginners to heel because you will do so many right turns, one after the other. But keep at it. The right turns really force your pup to pay attention; he doesn't have to pay nearly as much attention to you walking in a straight line, so throw him a few curve balls.

In addition to using the oval pattern, stop occasionally. As you slow for the stop, gather up the lead and prepare your dog to sit. You should only have to actually push him into a sit for the first two days. Each time, be sure to give the command, and then quickly praise your puppy. If he already knows the sit command, do not make physical contact. Simply repeat the command until he sits. For the more stubborn pup, it helps to lean over him while you give the sit command. As he looks up and finds you towering over him, you are in a very dominant position and he will usually slide right into a sit. Praise him immediately. If he does not sit, do not be afraid to give him an effective correction. With the correction, tell him, "No, sit!" Praise him highly when he does.

Make sure your pup is actually sitting. Some of the smaller dogs are sneaky. I had a Wirehaired Dachshund that would give me these really sheepish looks when we came to a corner and he sat. I finally realized that he wasn't actually sitting, the little sneak. He was so stubborn that he was faking his sits, crouching his hindquarters down. He was so close to the ground anyway that it looked like he was sitting. Finally, I had to start stepping out to my right to see if his derriere was actually on the ground.

You may be thinking, "Well, he stopped and squatted. Isn't that enough?" No, it's not. It wasn't good enough for him to go through the motions and almost sit. If I had let him win, he would have learned to push further and further until he didn't obey at all. Especially with stubborn breeds, like Dachshunds, it is important for you to show your dominance and win. In Rusty's case, he was also going through housetraining while he was training—and he did not think he needed to go outside to potty, either! What if his owners had allowed him to just pretend to go outside, but really do his business inside?

The point is: Follow through. Be consistent and persistent. And keep your pup focused on you. While you are training your puppy, do not allow him to sniff or stray. For those of you who have tracking dogs like Bassets or Bloodhounds, it will be more difficult because

When you are training your dog to heel, you should walk in an oval pattern using right turns. Here, Darby starts out comfortably, with slack in the lead and her chest level with the trainer. The trainer then exaggerates the motion of turning right, using lots of talking and praise to keep up Darby's enthusiasm. When the dog falls behind, she gives her a light correction forward and an encouraging command, "Darby, heel! Good girl!"

they have very strong instincts to keep their noses to the ground. But it can be done. Consider breed characteristics; for example, in this case, tracking dogs are bred for the sole purpose of sniffing things out, dashing ahead, and leading their owners forward. Now, suddenly, you're saying "Fido, Heel!" Fido asks incredulously, "What?" He looks around at the other tracking hounds that are shaking their long ears back and forth, feeling sorry for the silly human who is so clueless. "What did he tell you to do? Heel?"

Imagine if I told you that you were no longer allowed to sleep. It would be ridiculous. Sleep is so important. You would decide I wasn't competent to be advising you, and you would ignore me. So would your dog. You need to always establish yourself as the pack leader, the person in charge. For this reason, giving your dog the okay command is very important. Insist that Fido heels and that he does not sniff while you walk. Make him go through his paces of basic obedience. The reward then when you say "Okay," is that he gets to mill around the park sniffing all the wonderful smells life has to offer. He will learn to work for you when you require it because he knows he will be rewarded.

Another way to keep your pup focused on you during this 15-minute session is to make sure he has eliminated before the lesson begins. You don't want any distractions; his mind should be on you. Do not allow him to do anything in this session besides sit and heel. When he becomes distracted, correct him and tell him to heel. If he does not respond to the corrections, you are not correcting properly. (Refer to the correction instructions in the previous chapter.)

Your pup should respond immediately when you snap his collar. Every time you begin to walk, begin with the command, "Fido, heel." Be sure that you say his name before you give the heel command to catch his attention and call him along with you.

I have seen trainers who do not communicate. My experience is that their dogs do not learn as quickly, nor do the trainers have the kind of rapport with their puppies that they should. Dogs learn so much more quickly when they are praised, encouraged, and fairly and consistently disciplined. They begin to have confidence in what they are doing and to enjoy themselves.

Sosi, my little pound puppy, is a good example of how dogs gain confidence through training. When we began our sessions together, I had to pick a completely isolated area and work very slowly with her. She was very insecure. She cowered and whined every time we worked as though she had been abused. (Sosi had been abandoned when the animal shelter picked her up, so I know very little about her past, except that she shows all the signs of an abused animal.) I took it slowly and praised her and loved her every time she completed a sit. Remember to be careful how much enthusiasm you use when you praise a beginner, or she may become too excited with the praise and break the "heel." And you will, in effect, have set her up for a reprimand.

Over a period of five or six days, I saw Sosi's tail pick up, and she got more of a prance in her step. Because I suspected she had been abused, I touched her a lot during the sessions. As we heeled, I would reach over and pat her head, lightly flick her ear, or tap her nose. She grew to understand these were signs of affection and praise. Finally, she began to enjoy our sessions, and when she was praised, her chest swelled. Like most puppies, she loves to please.

While you are heeling with your pup, you should be able to walk the pace you want to, not the pace your pup wants to, and turn right or left as you please, without tripping over your dog. The biggest problem in this area is the left turn. The dog is ahead of you just enough that if you attempt a left turn, you end up turning directly into his side. So, let's talk about left turns.

Left Turns

In preparation for the left turn, gather up the lead as much as possible without pulling the chain. As you raise your right leg to step, pivot on the ball of your left foot, swinging your right knee in front of your dog. You are going to have to practice this one. Your knee should bring the dog to an abrupt halt. If your knee bumps into his face or shoulders, he is entirely too far ahead of you. Have patience. If you practice this exercise enough times, he will begin to watch for your leg to swing in front of him and will naturally fall back into a proper heel position.

Practice left and right turns at different paces. Stop and do a sit periodically. *Every time you reach a curb, do a sit.* When you begin to walk again, say "Fido, heel."

TRAINING: PHASE TWO

At this stage, you will introduce two new signals to your dog and demand automatic sits. By now, as you slow to stop, your pup should anticipate a sit. If you stop and he does not sit, immediately lean over him. Repeat the command to sit. He knows better at this point. You are being tested to see how much you really want him to sit. If, with the verbal correction, he does not sit, give him a physical correction and command, "No! Sit." It is important to note that if a second physical correction is needed, you then need to back up to Phase One. If your pup has not perfected the very basic sit, you have rushed the

When teaching the stay command, sweep your left hand in front of the pup's eyes while giving the verbal command, "Stay!" Once your dog is in position, you can use your left hand as leverage on the leash. The instant the dog breaks the command, step in and pull the lead taut. Repeat the command and put her back into the sit position until you release her.

training. Don't worry, though; all dogs don't move at the same speed. Your pup will get it. If your dog knows the command and has been doing fairly well but is just being stubborn on this day, perhaps your correction was not effective. Reread the instructions on corrections carefully.

Continue to practice the heeling exercises, turning left and right and varying the paces. Include stops and sits. Now, let's try something new. Once the pup is sitting, open your left hand and, with your palm facing the dog, slowly move it in front of his eyes from left to right. Keep telling him, "Stay. Good boy. Sit. Stay." This is a new exercise for him, and he may become insecure again. Reassure him. Repeat yourself to the point of exhaustion, if necessary. Do not walk away from your pup at this point. Have him sit and stay for a minute. Once this is completed, begin to walk again and command, "Fido, heel." Do not forget the verbal command. Every time you begin to walk, remind your dog to heel with a verbal command. Try to vary your walking patterns and the paces so that he won't get bored. Be sure that you don't get bored, either. Do not let your pup sniff or stray.

Continue the stay commands, and remain close to your pup. Your close presence will give him confidence, but will also remind him to stay. Repeat the stay command over and over again so that he will learn it well. As he becomes more reliable with his stays, increase the length of the sit/stay command. Check the workout guide to see how long your pup should be able to perform the stay.

The Down Command

Once you have your dog placed in the sitting position, give the command, "Down." Use a firm voice, because dogs are often more resistant to this command than any other. Again, do not shout at the dog. Your voice should be monotone. As with the sit command, gather up your leash so that you have more control over your pup. Use your left hand to push slightly and gently on your dog's back, while your right hand (also holding the leash) pulls gently on his front paws. As you are guiding him into a down position, reassure him, "Good boy, good down." It is important to repeat the actual command as much as possible. Just like humans, the more your dog hears it, the easier it is to learn and remember. And just like children, the dog may not actually hear the command, so keep on saying it over and over again.

With a smaller dog, it really does work better if you squat down beside him and use your forearm for leverage. With your left forearm resting on his back, pick up the slack in the lead in your left hand and gently push down. Tell him, "Down," and put tension on his collar. It

To give the down command, sweep your left hand in front of the dog while telling him, "Down!" You may have to apply pressure to the lead by using your left hand to press down. Here, as Kodi goes down, he is praised, "Good down, Good boy!" Once he is in position, he is reminded to stay.

Instead of getting into a wrestling match with a more stubborn dog, use your foot on the leash as leverage to pull your dog down. Once he is in position, give him lots of praise.

is easier on the dog than tugging on his neck. Gently push, giving the command, "Down."

Either technique is quite effective with smaller or more passive dogs. However, if you have a large and/or stubborn dog, it may not be that simple. If your dog is resisting going down, use the following trick: With your dog sitting on your left side, raise your left foot slightly and slip the lead underneath. You are going to use your foot as leverage. With the heel of your left foot firmly on the ground and your toes lifted up slightly, pull the lead so that it is taut. Now, using your left hand, gently push between your dog's shoulder blades (a pressure point) to coax him down while you pull the lead with your right hand. Be sure to give the command, "Down," as you push his shoulders with your left hand and pull the lead with your right. On our first day of class, one of my students, Rufus, and I had a standoff for several minutes. He locked his mighty Newfoundland shoulders and refused to go down. Rather than lose patience or wrestle him, I used my foot as leverage with the lead. I applied pressure to his shoulders and kept the lead taut. Eventually, he became tired and slowly sank into a down. The minute I felt him giving, I began to praise him and repeated the command, "Down."

At this early stage, do not make staying an unhappy event. Make your pup stay for about 30 seconds. If you must, keep your hand on his back and continue to tell him what a good boy he is for going down. The feel of your hand on his back may be very reassuring to him, particularly if he is insecure. Be careful, because your puppy may squirm and wiggle around until he has managed to do exactly what he had in mind—get up. The minute he begins to squirm, correct him verbally. Tell him "No, stay. Good stay. Good down. Stay, down." If he continues to wiggle, correct him and sound a little disgusted. Tell him "No" and "Down" in a firm voice.

During the next few days, remember these few things: Your pup is allowed to sniff while he is in a down, but he is *not* allowed to crawl over to something to smell it or to investigate it. He can only stare at it. He is to stay in the very spot you put him. If he suddenly gets up, correct him and take him back to the very spot you placed him. If he begins to crawl on his belly, correct him and take him back to the spot you placed him. Once your pup realizes that you are committed to this command, he will begin to work with you. Again, remember that all dogs are different. Some may respond immediately, while others may put up more of a fight.

Next, you will teach the hand signal for the down. Use your left hand (as you did with the stay), palm facing down, and make a gesture slowly to the ground. While you use this hand command, be sure to repeat the verbal command. Do not face your dog while you give this command. By facing him when you bend over to give the "down" motion, you are inviting him to break the stay and run toward you. Facing him is part of the gesture you will make during the recall commands. *Always* keep your left side to your pup while giving the stay and down commands. As the two of you progress, you will be able to use this hand signal from a distance (even without the verbal command in more advanced training).

No matter how good the workouts seem to go, do not stray from your practice schedule. If you move along too quickly, you may shake your pup's confidence and, as a result, cause damage to the training program. The best trainers always have a great deal of patience with their dogs.

Check your workout guide and be sure to vary your exercise programs. By this time, you need to think about finding a new workout area for new sights and new distractions, even if you have to pile into the car to get there. Good luck, and remember to keep your left hand off the leash, praise your pup, and watch his tail.

When giving the down command, always stay to the puppy's left, and use your left hand, palm facing down, while using the verbal command. After a few sessions, your dog will go down smoothly.

TRAINING: PHASE THREE

Congratulations! You have made it to Phase Three, which means the rest is "as easy as pie." According to your workout schedule, you and your companion are able to do sit/stays, down/stays, heels with left and right turns, and automatic sits when you stop. That is great! Now you are going to focus on these commands and the recall from a distance of six feet. Six feet may not seem like much now, but remember that everything builds on the parts that came before. *It is important not to skip anything!*

First, let's tackle the sit/stay and down/stay commands from this distance. Your dog has really built his confidence up to this point, and he knows what you want. That is the key to successful training. The dog wants to please his owner, and once he knows what you want, he will usually deliver.

When teaching the stay, be sure to give your dog the corresponding hand signal and reassuring praise. However, be careful not to become too animated, or you may encourage him to break position. When the exercise is over, walk to him and release him from the stay, giving lots of praise.

Sit/Stay and Down/Stay

Place your dog in a sit and use a hand signal for the stay. Until now, you have remained by his side while training. Now, slowly, step away. Not too far, just a little step. If your pup moves with you, that's okay. Remember, this is new for him. Correct him and take him back to his original position and tell him to stay. Be sure to give him the hand signal. Visual aids for dogs are very important at this point in training.

If your dog is nervous or cannot seem to hold a stay, use your left hand as leverage on the lead. Place the lead between your thumb and index finger and make it taut so that the moment he starts to move, you are able to correct him verbally and simultaneously tighten the lead on his neck. This will keep him in a sitting position. When he becomes still, praise him and repeat the stay command over and over again. As he grows more confident, you may loosen the lead and slowly move farther and farther away until you are at the end of the lead. This will not happen in the first few days. It will take time for your pup to gain the confidence to stay as you move away from him. Be patient. It *will* happen.

At the end of Phase Three (as marked in the workout guide), you can begin to move about at the end of the lead. Move from side to side; your pup should remain still. Remember, if he is sitting, do not let him sniff the ground. He does not have to look at you the entire time, but no sniffing. If he is lying down, he may sniff but not crawl or move around.

Now, on to the down/stay. This works the same way. Once your pup is sitting, tell him to stay. Give both the verbal and physical commands. When you have stepped one full step away from your dog, turn your body so that your left side is to him and give the down command. Make sure that your voice is forceful. Often, I will make it more dramatic—with a long "Dowwwwn." Use a slow gesture with your hand. If he begins to creep toward you to do the down right next to you as he has always practiced (and there is a good chance he will), correct him. Say, "No," bring him right back to the original place, and repeat the command a full step away from him.

This time you are ready for him. The instant he creeps forward, step into him, cutting him off. Make the movement quick. Quite often, this surprises the dog and he will instantly lie down. That's good. Try it again and again. As he progresses, so will you. Take another step away and another, until you can give the signal from the end of the leash and he will go down. Sometimes, just when it seems that he really has gotten it, he will try creeping up on you again. It's a test. Do as you did in the beginning: Immediately step in and loudly (because he knows better) correct him, but *never lose your patience!*

How solid are your pup's stays? At the end of this phase, you should be able to put him in a down/stay or sit/stay, circle around him, and wiggle the lead all over the place. Gently snake the lead in a zigzag pattern while your pup is staying. The pressure will tug slightly at the collar. If the pup can ignore it and stay, he passes the test. If the workouts are a little shaky, stay with it another week. Do not progress until your puppy is ready. You should be comfortable with your corrections, and one correction should be sufficient.

By now, your pup is familiar and comfortable enough with the hand signal to be able to stay without the verbal command. Also, you should be practicing doing downs and recalls with hand signals only, which is good because it makes your pup watch you more during training. When dogs become comfortable with the routine of training, they often begin to drift off into puppy daydreams. They learn to listen for commands without actually watching the trainer. Using only hand signals forces your pup to watch you constantly.

After your dog's stays are really solid, there are some tricks you can try to make

Set your dog up with temptations while he's in the stay position. Eventually, he should be able to stay through any distraction, including wiggling the leash.

practicing advanced stays with your pup easier. Use a squeaky toy during your training session. Give your pup the stay command and then squeak the toy. When he has shown an interest in the toy, throw the toy to the side. If he begins to move quickly toward it, correct him verbally and remind him to stay. This exercise will strengthen his stays, not to mention his overall self-control. Don't try this until your puppy has moved on to advanced stays; this would be too much pressure for a pup in the beginning of training.

An even tougher test is to tempt the dog with food. When I was working at the training school, one of my favorite tests for advanced students was to take them to the ice cream shop. I would make them do a down/stay outside while I went indoors to buy an ice cream cone. (Of course, the dog I took with me was always on a long lead, and I was watching closely the entire time.) Then, I would come back outside to eat my ice cream cone, and flick bits of ice cream just out of the dog's reach. If he broke his down/stay, I quickly corrected him back to his initial position. If he could resist the temptation, he was rewarded with my cone. Almost all of my advanced students mastered this test. All except for the Cupp's chocolate Lab, Dixie. (Yes, Dixie Cupp. I don't name them; I just train them.) Personally, I think Dixie's failing may have been the result of a genetic trait—the inability of chocolate Labs to resist chocolate chip ice cream. Whatever the reason, Dixie could not resist that ice cream. The temptation was

TEACHING BASIC OBEDIENCE • TRAIN THE OWNER, TRAIN THE DOG

just too much, and she would leap—quivering and squeaking—on that ice cream and devour it. Oh, well. We can't all be perfect.

The Recall Command

Next, let's try the recall command. From the sit or down position, put your pup in a stay and go to the end of the lead. Once at the end, turn and face your dog. This is the only other time when giving commands that you say your pup's name, "Fido, come." This command is very important. How many of you have become so agitated when your dog would not come that you began screaming the pup's name? "Fido, you come here right now!" you scream, your voice sounding like you are going to beat the dog to death when you get your hands on him. Now, stop. Would you come to someone like this!? Boy, I tell you what—I'd be running the other way. When you call your pup, make sure your voice is very upbeat and happy. You really want him to come to you.

When you call your dog, lean over to the left. You will see what I mean when you start applying this. When you call your pup, he will automatically head for your right, his left. But you want him to be on your left. By leaning over to your left, he will be more inclined to run straight to you. While he is coming toward you, take a few steps backward and praise him as he comes. The reason for walking backward is that it helps your pup turn around for his sit, as well as giving him incentive to trot toward you. Again, you may have to use your left hand as additional information to ease him over to your left side. When his nose almost touches your leg, take a small step forward. This forces him to fall into a heel at your left side. Once you have taken that small step, stop. As soon as your pup has turned around, he should fall into an automatic sit. Try it again and again. This is the most difficult command for the owner to execute. You will feel very clumsy with the lead, reeling it in as he moves in. Practice.

Max, the Golden, flew through all of his basics until we got to this command. I watched as his owner, Marilyn, would call him to her. Max would immediately stand up and stare at her. As soon as Marilyn began to walk backward a few steps and call him, Max would trot forward. It had not been clear to him what she wanted when she stood still. It was only when she walked backward that he would run to her. Now, at graduate off-leash level, he knows better. Marilyn had to *show* him what she wanted first—to come when she called, even when she stands still. Every lesson builds on another.

Remember to keep your voice upbeat when you call your pup. Lean over to the left to *show* him where you want him to go and step backward. Call, lean, and step. Once your dog becomes more confident, eliminate the backward steps.

The recall hand signal should always be given with the left hand out to the side while saying the dog's name, "Kodi, come!" Make your tone of voice happy and excited, and follow with lots of physical affection and praise when the dog reaches you.

Check Yourself

Don't forget to track your own progress along the way. Some things to check periodically are:

- Are you checking the collar if you have a long-coated dog? It is important to remember that with the long-coated breeds, your dog's hair can get caught up in the chain, preventing the two rings of the collar from falling together. The collar will then stay tight after a correction, which works against you. Check it by running your fingers around the collar and freeing the hair.
  - Are you letting your left hand guide the lead?
  - Are you using hand signals?
  - Are you working the dog on schedule?
  - Are you working the dog at all?

Exercise Drills

Your workouts should now consist of sit/stays and down/stays of up to five minutes, dozens of recalls, and heeling at varying paces with distractions. Try walking very, very slowly, and then begin running. This is a perfect setup, because the minute you begin to run, the pup thinks that there are no more rules. The minute he breaks the heel, correct him and try several left and right turns. Try the running drill again. This is such an important drill, because all too often I have seen dogs break training when the owner has to run. And I have seen some people get injured when the pup forgets himself and runs in front of the owner.

Try left and right turns at varying paces. Make sure your pup does not drag behind you on the right turns or that he is not too far ahead of you on the left turns. When he is in a stay, walk all the way around him. Stand behind him. Here's a little favorite of mine: Stand off to the side of your pup and find something like trash, a leaf, or a rock and begin to kick it in front of him—close enough to drive him crazy, but just out of his reach. If he can resist the object and stay, the two of you are cooking. Congratulations! Remember to praise your pup highly.

It is these kinds of exercise drills that will make your dog more reliable and stable. While I was training at Olde Towne, my number-one teaser was to have the resident cat, Northeast, walk by a dog in a stay. When Northeast was feeling particularly like a cat, she would walk right under the dog's nose and slap the dog with her tail. (Of course, this could have only been done by a cat like Northeast—not all cats are up to this test either!) Some dogs fell

Practicing your commands on a consistent schedule will make your dog more reliable and stable.

apart, and some held on like troopers and were greatly rewarded. Those that failed were set up again and again until they were able to stay. One Golden that was an infamous cat chaser in his neighborhood was finally able to stay, although he trembled and whined as our cat strutted past. When she had gone, I told him it was okay and gave him a hug. I found that he had had an accident on the floor, but he passed the test. What a good pup!

Many of my clients would often say, "My God, that cat has a death wish." I would tell them that she knew the trainers would never allow any harm to come to her—we were too quick, and she had complete and total trust in us. Here's the point: When you train with animals, any animals, you build a kind of rapport that you cannot get any other way. You begin to trust each other and you learn to read each other's body language. You can almost predict what the other is going to do. How do you improve on this? Keep trying to test your dog. Change paces, quicken the turns, and test his stays with temptations. Never let him get bored. Unfair? Hardly. He will test you all the time. And you will both be the better for it.

TRAINING: PHASE FOUR

Before you begin this phase, take a moment to reflect on how far you have come. You have worked hard and now is the time to reap the rewards—both of you. How many times have you seen people in the park playing Frisbee™ with their dogs or throwing balls into the water for their dogs to catch and been envious? Now, it's your turn to really enjoy your dog. Begin teaching him new things, beyond basic obedience. Try playing fetch or try swimming.

Once your dog is confidently able to heel, come, sit, go down, and stay on command on a 6-foot lead, you should repeat the commands using a longer 15-foot lead.

(*Be careful!* Many people don't know that *all dogs can't swim.* Barrel-chested dogs, for example, have to learn to make themselves long when they swim. Many Rottweillers try to paddle horizontally and simply sink. And, jumping into the water to save a panicked, sinking Rottie is not something you want to do.) Begin to explore new things with your pup as you both learn more and more about obedience training. You will both be the better and happier for it. Okay, now on with the show!

To prepare for this phase, you need to buy a 15-foot lead. Again, it should be nylon or cotton web with a sturdy clasp. Practice reeling in the 15-foot lead without your dog attached to it. Lay the lead out at length in your living room and, as quickly as you can, reel it in as if you had done the recall command. Until now, you have only been working with and reeling in six feet of leash. And believe me, that extra nine feet makes a big difference. I cannot tell you how many owners have completely tangled themselves in the lead when the dog rushes in and suddenly there is more lead to deal with than there ever was. It is fun to watch a dog laugh and dance around his tangled owner, although the "master" is usually not very amused.

According to the schedule, when you enter this phase, your dog should be able to confidently heel, sit, stay, down, and come on command. You should feel good varying paces and feel good with the leash. Are you still watching your left hand? Are you certain that you are using your dog's name only with heel and come commands?

In this phase, everything is to be repeated—but with a 15-foot lead. Not the whole lead at first. During the first week, use no more than eight to ten feet. Big deal, you're thinking. Do not rush your dog or yourself. This is a lot more lead to reel in with the recall. If you call him in from 15 feet and you lose control of the lead, your pup will be running circles around you, and you will have successfully blown a recall. Your pup will remember that one, too. I guarantee it.

Practice reeling in the lead without your dog until you feel comfortable with the movement. Now try it fastened to the dog. Go ahead and put him in a sit/stay position in the house and try the recall. It was pretty sloppy, right? That's okay. Although it will be a mess the first couple of times, it will soon become second nature to him and you.

Heels, Stays, and Recalls with the 15-Foot Lead

When you are heeling with the 15-foot lead, do not allow more lead to hang down than you would with the 6-foot lead. Allow only enough to keep your pup comfortable, but enough for you to administer a good correction. Remember, your dog should always walk at your left side while heeling.

When you both feel good with this new lead, increase the length for downs, stays, and recalls until you are eventually working on the end of the 15-footer. Again, just as you did with the six-foot lead, vary the paces and mix up your commands. Practice the quick right and left turns. Use your voice sometimes, and use only the hand command at other times.

I had a student named J.R., a red Doberman, that advanced to off-leash training. From 50 feet away, I could throw up my hand and he would drop into a down perfectly. I threw my hand to my left, and he immediately sprinted to my side and fell into a perfect heeling sit. This was a dog who had tremendous self-control and confidence. And he could resist *all* temptation. I mention temptations because self-control is an extremely important quality in your dog. Not just because he will work better for you, but because he will be much less likely to put himself in danger by running into a street or doing something he shouldn't. Only through consistent training will this self-control happen. The 15-foot (and longer)

When doing a down from a distance, do not face your dog, because she may try to come to you. Notice that as the trainer gives the down command, she turns away from the dog, showing only her left side. If the dog stands up, the trainer can move quickly, blocking her path.

stays, heels, and recalls should be practiced over and over again with lots of love, praise, and physical affection. Sosi, Fido, and now Nala all fly to my side because they know they will get plenty of loving.

When your dog is in a down/stay at the end of the 15-foot leash, create distractions for him. Bring a ball and bounce it or kick a rock or can around. He knows by now that he is to stay; he knows that you are playing little mind games with him, but he has to stay. You should be learning to read his body language by now. You can tell when he is thinking about sniffing or when he sees a squirrel and is thinking about bolting; you can tell when he is daydreaming—and you can put a stop to it. If he is in a sit/stay and is staring dreamily down the street, whistle to him slightly or say, "Hey, pretty baby," in a sweet voice until he focuses on you again. Many times, the pup's first reaction after you've gotten his attention again is to stand up and come to you. Immediately say, "No, sit. Stay," and start over again.

The reason you create distractions for him and the reason you do left and right turns while heeling is to force your pup to pay attention to you, to read your body language rather than just listen. Another big payoff for you is that when you have a dog that watches you all the time and that is that tuned in to you, you also have an awesome watchdog. (Of course, you may have to protect him from the burglar, but he'll certainly let you know that a burglar is on the premises.)

My Doberman, Tasha, is an awesome watchdog and has chased off more than one burglar in her time. Okay, two. Our training sessions together made her a better dog and me a better owner. I am very aware of her body language and her of mine; we read each other very well. She knows when I don't like someone (although I don't show it). In fact, she will stand between me and a person I don't like, putting herself right in front of me. But she will stand next to someone I like to welcome them. We have learned a lot from each other and have a great relationship. After the training you and your pup have been through, you should be beginning to build this type of relationship.

Out-of-Sight Stays

By now, your pup's stays should be solid. He should be able to maintain a good five-minute stay without any distractions. So far, he feels confident in his ability to stay, but you have been in sight. Even when you walked around him, he knew that you were there. So, let's change that.

Do not do this drill in busy areas if you have an aggressive dog. Even though that may seem obvious, I am constantly amazed by what people do. Though your dog may be doing well

To set up the out-of-sight stay, make sure that you can see the dog but that he can't see you. Also, pick a place that is safe in case your dog decides to break his stay and wander off.

in the lessons, an aggressive dog has to be watched closely. *Always*. Do not risk someone else's dog—or worse, child—for this test! You must understand that while your pup is in an out-of-sight stay (and by the way, the out-of-sight is only for your pup; you should always be able to see him), people will come up to him and pet him. Again, if you have an aggressive dog, you should be reading the section on how to deal with aggressive dogs before you begin training. Then do the out-of-sight stays only in areas where no one else is around. If you have a very cute puppy, you should be prepared for the fact that people will come up to your pup saying, "Oh!" and wanting to pet him. In the beginning, your pup will leap up, a mass of tail-wagging and smiling happiness. Do not be angry (this is too much temptation for a young pup still in training), just correct him back to his down/stay position and start over.

To do the out-of-sight stay, place your dog in a down/stay near a car or bush, tell him to stay, and move around to the other side of the obstacle. The reason for a car or bush is that your pup can still see you through the bush or under the car. He may need that reassurance at first.

You will have him lie down for the out-of-sight stay so that, while you are watching him, if or when he tries to break the stay by standing up, you will have time to run out and correct him. This allows you more time, and you will find that he will feel more comfortable if he is in a down. It is very important, however, to place your dog where he cannot run into the street or run up to people on the sidewalk. (Just because you may have a friendly Labrador doesn't mean that a small child who is afraid of dogs will be happy to see him, nor would the owner of another not-so-friendly dog.)

If your dog does stand up and immediately race around, correct him back to the original position, and try again. This exercise is very important because it teaches your dog to have self-control and discipline, even when you are out of sight. When he can complete a five minute out-of-sight stay, you have succeeded. You will find that your puppy has gained the confidence to stay alone until you return.

If your pup is very timid and shy and prone to nip at someone if he feels threatened, do not do this exercise. People will automatically walk up and put their hands in his face. He needs more socialization, but only with you present. You are your pup's security blanket. With you gone, he might feel forced to protect himself. And, obviously, this is another reason I do not recommend that aggressive dogs do this exercise.

Try this for three or four lessons, then move on to something more difficult. For example, I love to take a dog into the city and find a store that has large front windows facing the street. I will put the dog in a down/stay and, still holding the 15-foot lead, walk into the store and peer out at him. Many times I will have to race out and tell him "No, down. Stay!" and repeat the command all over again. People will see him outside the store and talk to him or try to pet him, but he must stay. If he breaks, I race out and correct him. I have startled a lot of innocent people by bolting out of the building, booming a "No!" This is the best test for stays. You will see that people will be very cooperative with you (once you have assured them you are not screaming "No" at them). After several tries, your dog will be able to stay where you put him and have people talk to him and pet him. Usually, I encourage people to talk to my pups, and they are often happy to be part of the training process.

Finally, congratulations! It's been demanding and frustrating, but you stuck with it. This was a great accomplishment. Keep up the good work. As proud as you are of your pup, I assure you that the feeling is mutual!

Work-Out Guide: Phase I

MONDAY	TUESDAY	WEDNESDAY	THURSDAY	FRIDAY	SATURDAY
Heel	Heel	Heel	Heel	Heel	Heel
Sit	Sit	Sit	Sit	Sit	Sit

Getting Started:

Heel and sit

Heel with perfect left and right turns

Work-Out Guide: Phase II

MONDAY	TUESDAY	WEDNESDAY	THURSDAY	FRIDAY	SATURDAY
Heel	Heel	Heel, Sit	Heel, Sit	Heel, Sit	Heel, Sit
Sit	Sit	Stay	Stay	Stay	Stay
Stay:	Stay:	Down:	Down:	Down:	Down:
1 min.	1 min.	2 min.	2 min.	2 min.	2 min.

Notes:

This one-week phase includes stay, down, heel, and sit.

Spend the week perfecting these drills.

Remember to vary your pace.

Talk to your pup.

Watch your left hand.

If you lose patience, take a break. Keep the lessons fun and rewarding.

You are working toward a two-minute stay. Even if your pup breaks the stay 15 times during the 2 minutes, praise him when the time is up. Keep practicing until he is able to hold a two-minute stay without breaking.

If this phase takes longer than one week, that is okay. Do not move on until your pup's stays are solid.

MONDAY	TUESDAY	WEDNESDAY	THURSDAY	FRIDAY	SATURDAY
Sit	Sit	Sit/Stay	Sit/Stay	Sit/Stay	Sit/Stay
Stay	Stay	Down/Stay	Down/Stay	Down/Stay	Down/Stay
			Recall	Recall	Recall

Notes:

First Week

Remember that as you work on the sit/stay and down/stay, you should be able to gradually move farther away from your dog (still holding the lead). If he breaks the stay, move in closer and try the command again. He should not break the stay unless you have called him.

Use your voice and hand signal for the stay in a calm, reassuring way. You need to use the hand signal only once, but repeat the command over and over.

Second Week

Work on perfecting all the drills.

Vary your pace.

Use distractions.

You want to make sure that you and your pup are very comfortable with this set of commands. If you rush him at this stage, he will break his stays later on.

Make sure that he can stay for five minutes on a down and three minutes on a sit.

Part Three

HOUSETRAINING AND BEHAVIORAL TRAINING

LIVING WITH YOUR PUPPY

HOUSETRAINING

To most owners, housetraining is the first and most important kind of training that a puppy needs. Although paper training is a popular method, do not put down newspapers unless you want to train your puppy to go to the bathroom in the house. Many elderly people prefer this method with their smaller dogs, such as Dachshunds or toy Poodles. For them, it may be a lot easier to train their puppy to go inside, and the dog can be perfectly content with this arrangement. Otherwise, papers only offer an excuse to go indoors. Setting up a regular schedule to go outside is a better alternative.

From the very first day, you need to establish that the house is not a place where your dog can urinate. To do this, it is essential that you set up a feeding and walking schedule and *stick to it*. There are some basic rules for housetraining your puppy:

- Do not give your dog an unlimited supply of water.
- Do not free-feed your puppy or new dog; set a feeding schedule.
- Let the puppy go outside directly after he has eaten, awakened, or after play.
- Do not allow the puppy to have free, unsupervised run of the house. You can, while he is supervised, attach a six-foot lead to your puppy's collar. If you catch him destroying something or going to the bathroom, you can easily catch him by grabbing or stepping on the lead. If you have to chase him and it becomes a game, the lesson and correction are lost.

A regular feeding and water schedule ensures that you will have a good idea of when your dog will need to go outside to relieve himself.

Let's discuss these rules one at a time.

1) Water: When there is an unlimited water supply available, the puppy is able to "refuel" constantly, and you will have no idea when he will need to go out. It's funny, but puppies seem to have an excellent memory about the location of the water bowl, but not the front door. By monitoring water intake, you will soon be able to gauge when your pup last had something to drink and when he will need to be let outside.

After playtime, you may give your puppy a little water, but be sure to take him outside directly afterward. When he eats, give him a bowl of water as well. You may also give him a little saucer of water from time to time during the day or evening—but only when you are right there to watch him.

2) *Food:* The same applies to food. Ideally, your pup should be fed three times a day until he is five or six months old. Then, cut feedings back to twice a day. If the puppy does not finish all of his food, that's okay. Do *not* leave it down for him to finish later. You may not be there to take him outside later on when he needs to go. It is more confusing to the dog if there is no set feeding schedule. Shortly, I will show you a sample schedule that has proven to be very helpful in housetraining pups. It's the working person's guide!

3. *Letting the Puppy Out:* It is generally true that approximately ten minutes after the puppy finishes eating, wakes up from a nap, or has settled down from a play session, he will have to go to the bathroom. If his pace quickens as he sniffs and moves in little circles, he is telling you he needs to go out. All pups are different, but this is the usual rule. Spenser,

Your puppy should be given plenty of time outside. If you consistently take him to the same area to eliminate, he will soon know what is expected of him.

my Rottweiler, always had to go to the bathroom twice in the morning, and I had him timed to go out at just under ten minutes after every playtime and evening meal.

4) Free Run: When you allow your puppy to run unsupervised, you are unable to monitor his behavior. He may crawl behind a chair or a dresser and go to the bathroom. It could be hours or days before you find the mess, depending on the size of your house or apartment. He could begin chewing on the leg of an antique chair and, again, it could be days before you see it. The owner's first reaction is to punish the puppy after discovering damage, but because it could have been done days before, the puppy will have no idea why he is being punished. Even worse than destroying carpet or furniture in the house, your pup could hurt himself. I had just begun puppy training with a Springer Spaniel in 1985 when his owner called to cancel our lesson. The puppy had been playing in the living room and bit into a cable television cord. He was killed instantly. This is terrible, but not so unusual. For your pup's safety, training, and the security of your items, monitor his territory.

By attaching a lead to your puppy in the house you can prevent accidents from happening. If you punish him after he comes to you, he will hesitate the next time. You must go and bring him back to the mistake. This is why the leash is so helpful.

Restrict your puppy to a safe area of your house until he is fully trained. This will make it easier for you to notice signs that he needs to go outside, as well contain any accidents that may occur.

It is important that you watch your puppy at all times when he is wearing a lead. It would be very easy for him to catch the lead on something and panic. Only use this method if you are able to be around him the entire time. If you cannot supervise your puppy, consider crate training, which I will discuss in the next section.

Here are some other things to consider when you are housetraining your puppy. Quite often, puppies or even older dogs will "scent mark" when they come into a new house. Chester, perfectly housetrained for five years, defecated on the floor of Mr. W.'s new home. Mr. W. was mortified. Chester was just making sure everyone knew this was his new house, too. Mr. W. was sufficiently shocked, and he booed and hissed Chester's behavior, sending him outside. Chester never did it again.

New puppies, however, will continue to do their business in the house until you teach them otherwise. Screaming is not teaching, and it isn't going to make your pup all fired up about going in front of you outside either. When you catch your puppy about to go, calmly ask, "Do you want to go out? Outside?" Repeat this over and over while you go outside. Some people say, "Go poop," or "Do your job." I had a Collie-mix student that would "poop" on command. Wait for the signs that your puppy needs to go out, like sniffing or running around in little circles. Once outside, wait patiently as he sniffs around to find the right spot, and always encourage him to go in the same area. This will help him figure out his "toilet" area. Repeat the command, "Go potty," or whatever you like. Then be sure to reward him for doing his job outside.

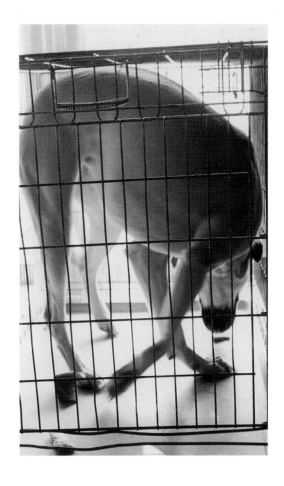

Crates can be used as a home away from home for your dog. Make sure your pup has just enough room in her crate to stand up, lie down, and turn around.

CRATE TRAINING

While you are at work or away on errands, you should find a way to confine your puppy. Most trainers recommend using a crate. I know it sounds cruel. I, too, thought so at one time. In truth, the pup begins to look at it as his room. Every time you leave, put the puppy in his crate. As long as you leave a few toys, a chew bone, and some sort of rug or blanket for him to sleep on, he will be happy. Be sure that the rug or blanket is washable. It will save you a lot of frustration during the first several months of housetraining.

At first, your pup may resist going to his "room." I would say that almost all puppies fight it for the first several weeks; then they begin to learn to walk in themselves on the command, "Go to your crate," or "Go to your place." The key to making him comfortable about his crate is to use a soothing tone and to repeat the command, "Go to your crate. Good boy. Good crate!" every time you put him in it. Some people say "room" instead of crate.

The crate should *never* be used as a punishment. If your pup chews a favorite pair of shoes or wets on the carpet, do not send him to his "room" as a way of punishing him. The crate is meant to reinforce good behavior, not to be used as a form of punishment.

Imagine training a 170-pound Bullmastiff to go into his crate on command. Boris and I fought for several weeks, but the end result is that he now thinks of his crate as his special room. The owners leave the door to the crate open and he walks in for naps, even during the evening when his people are home.

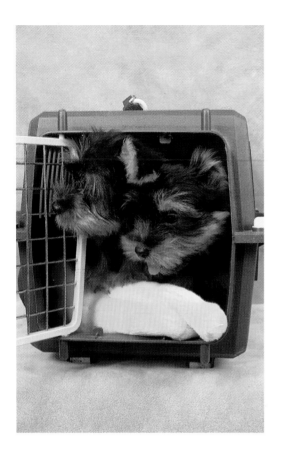

Teaching your puppy to accept his crate at a young age will help you in many different situations as he matures.

The importance of crate training goes beyond housetraining. What happens if you're dog needs to be boarded? If he needs to be crated for medical purposes or grooming? If he needs to fly on an airplane? You don't want an already unsettling experience made more traumatic for your dog. So teaching him to accept crates is a good long-term plan.

For those who are too uncomfortable with the idea of crate training, I suggest buying a baby gate and blocking the puppy off in a small room. "Small" is the key. Why? Because a pup will go to the bathroom in the far corner of a room if there is enough space, but dogs do not like to urinate or defecate if they have to stay near it. That is why crates have been so effective.

The best room for you to use for training is the bathroom, and even that may be too large. A small room allows the pup to look around, poke his head out, and feel more a part of the house. And, for dogs like JoJo, a ten-month-old Dobie, this was the answer. JoJo was so destructive he literally destroyed the wire-mesh crate he was put in. In a span of four hours, he destroyed the crate and hurt himself in the process. When left alone with free run of the house, he did several hundred dollars worth of damage to a couch and saw to it that an entire room had to be re-carpeted. For a dog like JoJo, the safest thing for him—and the house—was to put him in a small room where he could not hurt himself (no cables or electrical wires within reach) or anything else while he was unsupervised. JoJo was given a soft bed and some chew toys and left in the utility room. (If he chews the bedding, try an old piece of carpet. If he chews that, take it out!)

A crate can be abused as a training device. As an example, I had a Tibetan Terrier student named Churchill (as I said, I don't name them, I only train them) who was going to the bathroom in his crate, and then turning around and eating it. His owner called me at work and asked me why this was happening. Sometimes this is a sign that there is something lacking in the animal's diet, but this was not the case with Churchill. I asked the owner approximately how many hours Churchill spent in his crate every day. She calculated it at about 15 hours a day. It varied, but she and her husband were crating him when they went to work and also during the night while they slept. Poor Churchill had learned that if he was going to have to stay in the crate for so long, he would just have to adapt by eating his own feces! Other, less clean dogs would simply resign themselves to lying in it. I think this is incredibly cruel.

There are two obvious alternatives to this situation. One, give the puppy away. If you do not have time for him, do not punish him by forcing him to live such a terrible existence. Two, cut down the crate hours. Remember, it is not supposed to be a punishment. A pup should not be in a crate any longer than absolutely necessary. Obviously, most people work eight-hour days. But experts insist that a dog should not be crated for more than four hours at a time. Have a neighbor come let your pup out if you are unable to come home at lunch time, or hire a senior to stop by in the afternoon or a child to come care for the dog after school.

Churchill's owners wanted to know what to do with him during the night. I suggested they use a baby gate to block off the bedroom and "puppy proof" the room. If the room is very large or you are concerned about the furniture, you can tether the pup to the bed, leaving about a ten-foot lead. Be sure to put down a little bed and some toys for him. Also keep in mind that the pup will soon be teething. Tether toys, nylon bones, and thin rawhide chew sticks will help eliminate the puppy's desire to chew on your antique chair leg. Often, I will suggest that owners put an old shirt that smells like them on the puppy's bed. The pup will snuggle up to the shirt because it smells like his owner, and he will sleep better. Remember, your puppy is a baby!

As for Churchill, once he was allowed to sleep in the room at night with his people, he could and would sleep the night through. After a month, they began to give him more run of the house during the day. Now, his crate stands open during the day, and he uses it for naps.

The best thing you could do is to take your dog everywhere with you on weekends and really let him run himself into the ground. It is my hope that the pup will be out of the crate

Dogs need lots of exercise for their physical and mental well-being. Make sure you provide your pup with plenty of time to expend all his energy.

within a six-month period. You are only crating him until he is reliable in the house alone. You very likely will always leave the crate out for him (with the door taken off), so that he can go in and out of his "room" as he pleases. He won't be confined there forever. (Tasha, my brave Doberman, is terrified of thunderstorms. During them, she seeks refuge in her safe "room.")

You may be thinking, "Wait a minute, this is much more work than I thought." Not really. Once you set up a reasonable schedule, it becomes very simple. In the sample schedule below, I use the typical workday schedule of 9 a.m. to 5 p.m. to give you an idea how to arrange your time.

Housetraining Schedule

6:30 a.m.   Take the puppy outside first thing.

7:00 a.m.   Feed and water the pup. Talk to your vet about the amount of food you need to feed him; give him one cup of water. Pick up the food and water in 20 minutes. Take your pup outside.

8:15 a.m.   Put the puppy in his crate or confined room. Leave for work. Have a nice day!

12:00 p.m.   If you are home or able to come home, it would be very beneficial to training if you could let the puppy out at noon and 3 p.m. (and feed him at noon).

3:00 p.m.   Take the puppy outside if possible.

6:00 p.m.	Immediately let the puppy go outside. Love, praise, and play with him.
6:30 p.m.	Feed and water the puppy.
6:50 p.m.	Let the puppy go outside.
8:00 p.m.	Let the puppy go outside.
10:00 p.m.	Let the puppy go outside.

On Saturdays and Sundays, try to stick to the schedule as much as possible. As I mentioned earlier, it will help your puppy acclimate to his new home. He will learn to anticipate mealtimes and walk times and adjust his needs accordingly.

DISCIPLINING YOUR PUPPY

Disciplining your pup is one of the most frustrating aspects of training. Believe me, I am always sympathetic to anyone who is trying to housetrain a puppy. However, a firm schedule and proper discipline make the training process go much more quickly, painlessly, and successfully.

The best way to discipline a puppy is to catch him in the act. If you find a mess that he is walking (or running) away from or one that is still "fresh," go get him and carry him back to the scene of the crime. Firmly push his face close to the "mistake" and scold him, telling him "No" and "Bad puppy." Do *not* rub his nose in it! Immediately carry him outside. You must do this every time, so that he is able to make the connection that outside is where he has to do this.

Elsie, a 200-pound Mastiff, was a submissive wetter. Every time her owner came home, Elsie would wet the floor. This would enrage her owner. He would punish her and throw her outside, tying her to the outdoor grill. He called one afternoon livid because Elsie had torn the very expensive grill right out of the concrete and was, as we spoke, running around the yard, dragging it behind her. Elsie was terrified to come to her master, sure of another punishment. It was unclear to Elsie what she had done in the first place, and now she was chained to a grill that chased after her. While her owners now laugh about how Elsie howled frantically, cutting turns left and right, trying to shake the evil grill, Elsie still won't come outside when the family barbecues.

When you take your puppy outside during the course of the day and he does go to the bathroom, praise him ecstatically. Praise him to the point of embarrassing yourself if anyone should hear you. The first time he hears your praise, he will be thrilled by the tone of your voice, and given time, he will make the connection. While I was housetraining Sosi, she got to the point that when she finished doing her "duty," she began to wag her tail. She was very

A firm schedule and the proper discipline make the training process go much more quickly, painlessly, and successfully.

pleased with herself, and she knew that as soon as she finished I was going to love her up and down. Praise goes a long way.

You simply must not, whether coming home to a mess after a hard day at work or even after finding a mess that is an hour old, punish your puppy for his mistake. He does not remember what he did an hour ago. Also, remember what we said earlier about not calling your dog to you to be punished. Never call the puppy over to get his punishment. Go to him and bring him back with you to the scene of the crime.

How you punish your pup is important for all his misdeeds, not just wetting. No matter how serious his crime, you must maintain control. I have seen many different methods used by owners and trainers to discipline their dogs. I have seen dogs get kicked, spanked, yelled at, slapped, hit with different objects, and pinched. Temper can slip away from even the best of trainers, but there is never an excuse for abuse of this sort.

Punishment—or better put, correction—should be considered in two steps. Step one is to control your temper. Screaming, becoming red-faced, throwing objects, or waving your arms about is not constructive discipline for your dog. The only result of this behavior is that he will fear you, and naturally, will want to run away from you. Many people say, "See that, he knows what he did; see how he runs away?" Of course he ran away. Most people would want to. Fear is not a constructive tool for training unless you are in the Marines. In training, losing your temper is a sign of victory for the dog and failure for you. Dogs will often try to test their owners. When you lose your temper, you lose control of the lesson.

Step two is to administer the proper discipline. Do not hit your dog with any object. Do

It is very important to remain calm and in control when disciplining your puppy. Proper discipline administered at the correct time will go a long way in defining your relationship with your dog.

not raise your voice or show any loss of control. Stay calm. There are many effective ways of disciplining dogs. One way is to sit the dog and gently swat him under the chin. Do not swat the dog from above. Keep your fingers together and connect with the underside of the dog's mouth, moving your hand forward and upward. Look at your dog: Remember, eye contact is extremely important with dogs. The other hand should hold the dog's collar so that he is unable to avoid the discipline. If he is able to slip away and it takes you ten minutes to catch him, the opportunity is lost. Young pups will frequently make a game of you chasing them or will be so worried about being caught that they will have completely forgotten about the dirty deed.

The actual correction has to be effective. I use my sister, Michelle, and her dog, Kinder, as another example. When Kinder and I are together, Kinder will not push me. She knows that I will give her a correction. However, when Kinder is with Michelle, Kinder pushes. Michelle administers corrections that could easily be misunderstood as pats. One good correction can replace ten mediocre or soft corrections.

Some trainers suggest grasping the dog on either side of his face and firmly shaking him once or twice while repeating your command, such as "No jumping" or "No barking." If you are consistent, your dog can build a fairly large vocabulary; that is, he will discern what it is you are trying to communicate. Dogs who are very sensitive about disappointing their owners are easily shamed, and that is by far the most productive discipline.

By grasping your dog's muzzle and staring him in the eyes, you have established eye contact between you and the dog. With some of the larger dogs, such as Newfoundlands and Rottweilers, it is easy to grab their jowls. With the smaller breeds, you can just as easily grab the collar and gently shake. Facing the dog as you shake him, lift him slightly off his front paws. This will command his attention. While you do this, scold him, using familiar commands.

Remember not to shout or lose your temper. A calm but firm tone combined with handling of his collar or jowls will most definitely get his attention. When you are holding his collar or jowls and standing over him, you are in a very dominant position. You will find that he will stare back at you at first, but will then look away. By looking away, he is submitting to you. When you let him go, remind him once more of what he has done. Tell him, for example, "No barking," in a stern voice and let him go.

Madison is a different story. Her owner and I were laughing about the fact that once a Newfie makes up her mind about something, that's it. For example, when Madison gets in trouble, her owner grabs her jowls as we discussed. Madison averts her eyes. Her owner then says to her, "Look at me. Madison, look at me!" Madison simply closes her eyes. Voila! The problem and the disappointed owner have disappeared! So, what does the owner do? He gently, but firmly, shakes her. Madison will roll her eyes around, avoiding eye contact. Sounds like a young teenager, right? For Madison, the only way to get through to her is to continue the hold until she sighs and gives in, usually falling into a down/stay. For this kind of behavior, the best thing her people could do is to make her do a down/stay in a "time-out" area.

Be firm, but fair, and be consistent.

SUBMISSIVE WETTING

Submissive wetting is a common problem among young or submissive dogs. Punishment for this kind of wetting can, and will, only make the problem worse. When you come home or when you are loving the pup, he may urinate with excitement. Puppies really have little control over their bladders, and if they are very excited to see you, they may wet. Owners who come home from a long day see this behavior a lot.

Nervousness can also cause this type of wetting. Perhaps the pup is afraid that he may be punished. I have seen this behavior with dogs whose owners come home, discover a mistake, and proceed to punish them. Think about it: the pup is nervous that he may be punished, but does not know why. He did not do anything wrong that he remembers, and he could not help the submissive wetting.

Remember Levi, the Pit Bull? Poor Levi felt the first thing that would happen to him when his owners came home was that he would be beaten. Five hours had passed since he made any mistakes, and he had no memory of anything except that when his owners came home, he would be hit. The result was that the submissive wetting only worsened. For several weeks, I had the owners walk into their house and act distracted. They would say a cheerful "Hello" to Levi, and busily straighten things up or move about until the pup had calmed down. Once Levi was calm, they let him outside and played with him. Eventually, Levi overcame his fear of being punished, and the owners learned the proper time to punish and praise Levi.

Submissive dogs that are dominated tend to suffer uncontrollable wetting. To illustrate, when you approach a dog to say hello, pet him, or even discipline him, think about your position and the position of your puppy. You are usually standing over him. This is very threatening, especially for a submissive personality, and the timid puppy will urinate while you stand over him. What can or should you do? Nothing. Ignore it. Most puppies will grow out of it. R.T., a Rottweiler, was a submissive wetter until he was about 10 months old. Suddenly, there was no longer a problem. However, had he been punished every time he wet, it could have developed into an ongoing problem. Puppy Rottweilers make semi-small messes, but adult Rottweilers make really big ones!

TEETHING AND DESTRUCTIVE BEHAVIOR

Destructive behavior often begins when a puppy is teething. The puppy, in search of something to soothe the pain, chews on wood because it feels good on his gums. This is the way bad habits are formed unless corrected. After he is through teething, a dog may chew due to boredom, restlessness, or habit. It is essential to catch this in the very beginning.

Teething usually begins at 10 to 14 weeks, although it can vary among individual dogs. Sometimes you can even see black and blue markings on the gum line. This is your clue to rush to the pet store for chewing toys. It is vital that lots of toys are accessible to the pup. Squeaky toys will help to entertain him, but you also need to have nylon-type bones or any hard surface toys for teething. It is important to mention that many experts warn that rawhide chews can lodge in the gumline or be swallowed whole, choking the dog.

Puppies have a physical need to chew, so provide your dog with plenty of safe chew toys.

Another good teething toy is a frozen wet washcloth. While your puppy chews on it, it numbs his gums and makes him feel good. This is also an excellent toy to leave your puppy with during the day while you are gone. It allows him to numb his gums and suck on the water while it melts, but does not give him too much water; it is ideal for the confined area.

While it is important to give your pup lots of toys, do not make the mistake of giving him an old shoe or sock as a toy. Many owners falsely believe that the dog will understand or can be taught the difference between an old useless shoe and your new and very expensive hightops or Italian pumps. Wrong. Do not give your pup any toy that resembles something you want to keep around. Chewing discrimination is up to you. You must teach your pup what is and what is not acceptable. This may mean spraying a chewing deterrent such as Bitter Apple on an old pair of shoes or socks you care nothing about and strategically placing them somewhere for your pup to find. Once he pounces, he will be sorry. (Bitter Apple can be found in most pet stores. It comes in a spray or paste form that is not harmful to your pet, but tastes awful.)

This may seem obvious, but be sure to keep your house "puppy-proofed." A puppy is an infant. At first, he is unable to determine what is okay and what is not. Help him out. Remove temptation or set him up with the chewing deterrent. When he takes something of yours in his mouth, say "Bad" or "No," take it out of his mouth, and hand him one of his toys. Even at the age of five and six months, he is still a pup (just like a toddler) and is bound to make mistakes. Leather shoes and belts are pretty hard to resist.

Chew toys and treats help keep your puppy's mouth healthy while keeping him busy and out of mischief.

You really want to teach your puppy not to chew anything but his toys. Something as seemingly harmless as pantyhose can be lethal to a puppy if he chews it. Once inside the stomach, pantyhose acts as a saw and shears the intestines. Be fair to yourself and to the pup and keep your house puppy-proofed until he is a reliable dog.

Be aware that, though it is unusual, there are some pups who will never be reliable. Kinder is a classic example. This dog seems to have suicidal tendencies. She has eaten pantyhose, bras, underwear, socks—you name it. She had to have intestinal surgery to remove a stuffed toy that she swallowed and couldn't pass. In fact, while she was still in critical condition and hooked up to an IV (being transported back to the emergency clinic), she tried to scarf down a greasy paper towel lying in the parking lot. Michelle managed to extract it from Kinder's mouth (Michelle has very fast reflexes now, thanks to Kinder), but the vets were dumbstruck. After that, they referred to Kinder as "Garbage Gut" and told Michelle sympathetically that some dogs just have some sort of imbalance that can't be trained out of them. They had, at the time, a Golden Retriever patient who kept eating bras and having to have them surgically removed. I've seen this behavior a lot. Garth, an Airedale, threw up underwear in my presence. While the owners were extremely embarrassed because of the type of underwear we were looking at (ahem), they didn't take his illness seriously. Six month later, he died of intestinal damage caused by pantyhose he ate.

Admittedly, most people would not have kept Kinder. For Michelle, her love for Kinder outweighed the inconveniences, and she has been able to adapt her lifestyle to accommodate Kinder's needs. But most people might be unable or unwilling to do so. Indeed, some people and dogs (just like people and people) are not compatible. Just as people divorce, so too will pups and their people; only too often, the people fair far better. That is why I caution you to be selective. Think through this partnership before you seal the deal.

While these cases are obviously extreme, it is important to remember that you can't assume your pup is reliable or has common sense. Only training and the test of time will give you the answer. You need to be prepared to go to whatever measures are necessary to protect your pup (and your valuables). Garth's owners, tragically, never learned this. Michelle has learned (and has trained her roommates) to never leave any socks or undergarments within Kinder's reach—not even for ten seconds. (The dog moves like lightening.)

To recap, you must discipline your dog for any kind of destructive behavior. Most dogs can be trained to stay away from anything but their own toys. The rules for punishing destructive behavior are similar to housetraining rules. You cannot punish the pup for the damage of something that may have happened over an hour ago. I often hear owners say, "He knew what he did. As soon as I walked in the room he was cowering." If I thought the chances were fifty-fifty that you were going to beat me without any reason every time you walked into the room, I would cower, too. If, however, you walk in on the act, respond immediately. Place one hand on the back of his neck and use the other to hold his muzzle. Look him in the eyes and tell him, "No, bad dog! No chewing! No!" Then bring him a toy that belongs to him and gently hand it to him. Do not throw it, or he will interpret the toy as part of his punishment.

When you see your dog destroying something, but he is far away from you, do not charge him. If he sees you coming, he is likely to take off running. If the chase goes on for too long, it can turn into a game. By the time you catch him, you punish him for getting caught, nothing more. He has forgotten about the ancient wood carving from Zaire to which he added his own impressions. Walk toward him, but do not make eye contact. Many times, I will hum to myself and look up at the ceiling or to the side. Eye contact is very threatening. Once I am close enough to grab him, I pounce. Tell him "No" and "Bad dog" and again, give him a toy that belongs to him. Make sure you are not yelling when you give him the toy.

If your pup has a chewing problem, use a deterrent such as a bitter-tasting spray on the things you don't want him to chew, and make sure that you have plenty of safe substitutes to give him.

If your pup is chewing particular items, you can set him up. I had a chocolate Labrador student named Coffee who loved to chew on pencils. I told his owners to soak the pencils in Bitter Apple and leave them out for Coffee to chew. True to form, Coffee chewed one of the pencils and got a nasty surprise.

After a short while, he was getting wise to the terrible tasting pencils, so he inspected them first. Then the owners would soak only half of the pencil. They would let the untouched side of the pencil hang off the edge of the table. When he did not smell any Bitter Apple, he pulled it off the table. As soon as it was in his mouth, he spit it out and shook his head. His owners would periodically set him up in this manner until he was completely cured. With the proper correction and consistency, your dog will be cured of bad habits, too.

BEHAVIORAL PROBLEMS

In many instances, the behavioral problems you may be having with your pup are reinforced by your actions. Not only must you learn to train your pup, but you may need to evaluate your own actions as well. You will have to learn how to properly react to your pup, whether he has done something good or bad. A classic appropriate response example comes from a Sheltie lesson I had years ago.

During our first meeting, Mrs. Wilson told me that her Sheltie's barking was driving her crazy. She had tried everything to control it, but it was getting worse. While we were talking, Austin ran to the window and started barking. Mrs. Wilson called him back and, as soon as he came to her, she said, "Good boy, Austy; be quiet and stay here. Good boy." A few minutes passed, and he ran to the window again, barking loudly. "Austin!" she yelled. Again, he ran over to her side, and she scratched his head and praised him. When she left the room, Austin confessed to me that he was doing exactly what he thought she wanted. He would run to the window and bark, and she would tell him what a swell guy he was for doing it.

Your words may mean one thing, but your actions can mean quite another. Unfortunately, most dogs have a limited vocabulary and do not know what you want until you *show* them.

Your tone of voice is very important. Several years ago, my sister came to visit during the winter holidays with Kinder and Kaiser. Michelle and I returned from a shopping trip to find a skirt, half eaten, lying in the middle of the floor and the likely culprit staring at us with wide eyes. Quietly, I turned to Michelle to see what she was going to do. She picked up the skirt and stomped over to Kinder and whispered, "Kinder, you are a very bad girl." She has a lovely, soft voice, so Kinder wagged her tail. Her mission was completed, and it was a job well done; Kinder was quite pleased with herself.

Tone of voice can work the other way as well. I have a lot of clients who have complained that their dogs will not come to them off-leash. They scream and scream, but the pup will not come. Now, tell me, would you come to this: "Rufus, get over here. Come here! You bad dog! Come here! Get over here right now!" I know I wouldn't. Remember this when we discuss destructive behavior.

Your tone of voice and actions have to fit the behavior, whether it is one you want to reinforce or eliminate. If your voice or your actions encourage bad behaviors or discourage good ones, you will only confuse your dog and further frustrate yourself. When you are not getting the intended reaction from your dog, you may want to reassess what you are doing and how you sound.

You must also take into consideration your dog's breed and what some of the behavioral characteristics of that breed are. I mentioned that once Rufus enjoyed his training, his true Newfoundland characteristics came out. This has a double meaning. Any trainer, any vet, any animal behaviorist can give the pros and cons on any breed. Rufus had his cons, but proper training brought out the pros. But we also must not dismiss behavioral problems just because they are common to the breed. Roxie is a Beagle and, as you may know, Beagles are barkers. So Roxie is allowed to bark her fool head off, much to the annoyance of everyone, while her owner sighs, shrugs, and says, "Well, she is a Beagle."

I also knew a family who kept their three Irish Wolfhounds confined to the garage for several hours a day. As a result, the dogs ate the garage door that led to the house—*ate* it. These are large dogs that need a great deal of space for unrestrained runs and are still used for hunting stags, wild boars, wolves, and coyotes. Of course, this is not to say that these dogs are not good indoor dogs; they are. They are very loyal, patient, and excellent with children. They have wonderful senses of humor. However, they need a lot of exercise, plus large areas to roam.

We should not accept behavior we don't like. Because she is a Beagle, we need to work that much harder to make sure Roxie doesn't bark hysterically at dinner time or when she is going for a walk. When Irish Wolfhounds or Jack Russell Terriers become destructive, we need to give them more exercise. Unconsciously, we allow a great deal of bad behavior to continue without correction. Understanding the heritage of your puppy should only make you more determined to work *with* the behavioral problems, not dismiss them. Trust me, they won't go away by themselves, and understanding the needs of your breed is important for everyone's happiness.

EXCESSIVE BARKING

So, you have a barker. I am so sorry! I know how frustrating that can be. But what kind of barker is he? Does he bark when he is alone? Many times, people will find out from their neighbors that their dog barks the entire time they are out. He is lonely or afraid. That is the simplest answer. Try leaving a radio or TV on for noise. This is often very soothing for the pup, particularly if he is young.

Entire packs of wolves howl to ward off approaching packs. They will sit and howl for great lengths of time to make sure other packs stay away. Imagine how your lone puppy feels; there is just one of him. He's got a lot of barking to do to make up for the rest of the pack.

Barking During the Day

If leaving a radio on does not work, you might try confining your pup to a smaller room if you have not already done so. Why? Because dogs will frequently bark out of nervousness or fear. Sometimes a big apartment or house is scary when dogs are alone. So they bark to hear themselves and to ward off any scary bad guys who might be lurking around. Confining your pup to a small room provides security and comfort. If this fails or if your dog is already confined, you may have to face the fact that you have an excessive barker. This is a hard trait to stop. But with persistence, you can change your dog's behavior.

First, try the "logic" method. Every time he barks, ask, "Who is it?" If there is someone there, acknowledge it, and then tell him, "Quiet." If you praise him for the barking, it will only get worse. But, if you recognize someone or something is there, he will eventually learn to give warning barks, and then settle down.

If he continues to bark, or simply barks at the wind blowing, tell him "Quiet," and gently hold his muzzle. "No, quiet." Repetition is the key. If you catch it in time, this works quite well for the young pups.

For older dogs that now have a set pattern of behavior, you may also try the squirt-gun method. If you have repeatedly told him "Quiet," and he keeps barking, squirt him with water. But, remember to always explain what you want. "No, quiet" or "No barking." Pause.

Some breeds are more predisposed to barking, but there are several ways you can train your dog to control his natural urges.

If there is still barking, squirt. As you squirt, say, "No! Quiet."

Third, there is the shake-can method. Get a coffee can. Empty it, fill it with about 20 pennies, and tape the top down. When you tell your pup "No barking!" and he continues, shake the can loudly at him. Repeat your command, "No barking!" over and over again. The shake can makes a terrible noise when you shake it. (But be sure to tape the lid down so the pennies won't fall out. Believe it or not, if the pennies fall out and the dog sees them, the can loses its threat.) *Warning: Do not do this with a skittish dog!*

My parents' Lab, Ziek, becomes hysterical whenever anyone leaves the house. He had been left by three families before my parents adopted him and is terrified of being left again. Anytime someone leaves the house, he begins shrieking (believe me, this dog doesn't bark, he shrieks). My parents keep a shake can by the door, which they pick up when he barks. Even as they are bending down to pick up the can, he is running up the stairs away from the can. For most dogs, this method would work. For Ziek, the nut, he simply runs farther away from the can and continues barking. He thinks if he just stays away from the can, he'll be safe. Because he runs, the squirt gun is the perfect solution. Also, training is giving him more confidence, and he will eventually calm down as he becomes more convinced that my parents will not leave him.

If your dog is barking while you are gone, set him up. Leave the house as you normally do, but wait outside or around the corner so that he thinks you have really gone. Get ready with your can. The moment he begins to bark, run into the room shaking the can. "No barking! No!"

I would like to add a reminder: A barking problem is one reason why finding the right breed is so important. Some breeds are notorious barkers. Talk to your vet about this. It may very well be that you have a breed that just loves to bark. What this means is that you will have to work a bit harder to break the barking trait. You must be consistent. If you tell him "No barking!" you must follow up. Remember the barking Beagle? He can be trained to bark only for "emergency" reasons, but you must always make the corrections when he slips up. What are barking emergencies? Obviously, intruders or someone strange lurking around your home. In my house, there are a few more. A treacherous squirrel lurking about or a menacing cat is a reason to bark. No, I don't let them bark endlessly, but I do let my dogs express themselves. When Nala and Sosi play, I allow them to bark at or with each other. Other than that, if we are in the house and one of them should bark, we all take notice. They don't "bark wolf," so we know someone must be close by.

Believe it or not, by teaching dogs to control themselves (in barking), we teach them to discern noises. What is a noise from a family member and what is a "strange" noise? Ziek, the wonder barker, barks at any and every sound he hears in his house. If someone bangs a can against a kitchen counter, accidentally lets the door slam, or bangs a drawer shut, Ziek is up and shrieking. In my home, my daughters Kerri and Katie play house, knocking on their bedroom door. Nala and Sosi remain unphased. They know it is just their little girls.

Some people turn to "bark collars" that administer an electric current to the dog each time he barks. Personally, I have a fundamental problem with the idea of shock therapy but, besides that, what if there is real need for him to bark—to warn you of something or warn someone else away? A bark collar will prevent him from doing so or at least make him more hesitant. This is unfair and might be dangerous for you.

Other people have had their dogs' vocal chords removed. Get rid of the dog and adopt a cat if you are considering this procedure! It is amazing to me that some vets will even do this operation!

Another effective set-up tactic involves putting a long lead (15 or 30 feet) on your dog. (This will only work if he is confined to a crate.) Fasten the lead to his chain collar. Trail the lead out the doorway. When he believes that you are gone, he will undoubtedly bark. When he does, yank the lead to give him a correction and yell, "No barking." Again, if this is done enough times, you will be able to leave the lead on him and go out. He will think that someone is at the end of his lead, and he will not bark. *But be sure only to leave the lead on him when he is confined to the crate, and wearing a flat collar*—not a choke chain. As time goes on and you are confident that he is not barking, remove the lead. If it starts up again, begin the procedure again. This method has been most effective with dog owners who live in apartment buildings. After some time, neighbors report they hear an occasional "woof," but nothing more. If you come home and find that your dog has chewed the leash he is wearing or was wearing, treat it with Bitter Apple to discourage chewing.

Barking While You Are Home

If your dog is barking while you are home and does not respond to your no barking command, use the "logic" method, the squirt gun, or the shake can. You also can buy a short lead or cut an old one so that it barely touches the ground. You do not want it to get caught up in furniture or trip him. When he barks, grab the lead and correct him, using the verbal command as well. An additional deterrent is the faithful Bitter Apple spray. Every time he barks, tell him, "No," and squirt a little bit into his mouth. After several episodes of this, he will take your command very seriously.

Take note, however, that he will probably try to run from you as soon as he barks. He figures you can't squirt him with the Bitter Apple if you can't catch him. If you can't catch him, you can squirt him with a squirt gun—with water, of course. You may want to trail a lead from his collar when you are in the house and trying to break this habit. Always take the lead off when you leave the house; it does not take long for dogs to tangle themselves up and panic. They can inflict serious damage on themselves. Always be sure to watch your dog when the lead is on.

Barking While Outside

Hello, garden hose! It is the easiest, most effective way to catch your barking pup's attention. You may also use the lead-trailing method. You may need to tie several leads together to make sure the end of the lead reaches the doorway so that, as soon as your dog begins to bark, you can grab the lead and correct him. "No barking!" Consistency is the key. This method is more difficult than the garden hose, but if you are able to do it, it is very effective. Again, if you have a breed that is known for barking excessively, you have more work ahead of you, but if you stick with it, you will see progress.

Barking at Other Dogs

Lady and Philipe were two Shih Tzu who loved to bark at other dogs while they were on leash. They fed off of each other's behavior, barking bravely at all the dogs who passed by. Small breeds, particularly, bark to warn other dogs away or to show how tough they are. As soon as Lady and Philipe were separated, the barking stopped. Together, they figured they made one mean dog. The only way to stop this barking in the initial stages of their training was for their owner to carry a shake can. As soon as the dynamic duo began to bark, the owner shook the can and reminded them, "No barking." Consistency is the trick. Lady and Philipe responded quickly to the shake can. As they progressed in their training, they learned that while they were on leash and working, they must not bark at other dogs. Each time they did, even if they growled, they would be corrected.

Sophie, the Golden Retriever, is another dog who is tempted to bark. While she is working, she knows better than to bark at another dog, but if she is taking a leisure walk with her mistress and they pass another dog, she wants to bark. Knowing this, her owner pulls Sophie into an automatic heel, and Sophie knows that it is time to work. No barking is allowed.

Control is so important, because you may know your dog's temperament and what he is likely to do, but you can't predict the actions of the dogs you pass on the street. As long as you have control over your dog, you may usually pass with ease. When I walk with Tasha, I often pass a man with a Boxer that barks insanely at us, straining at the end of his leash to break free. His owner barely has him under control. Tasha ignores the Boxer and we continue our walk, but imagine if she behaved the same way. Tasha's response would be all that Boxer needed to pull his owner right over and pounce on us.

DIGGING

What is the first thing a dog does before he is about to dig? He sniffs. If you have a digger, like I did, you always have to stay on top of him. There are diggers by nature, and dogs who dig because they are bored or want out of the yard.

There are several ways to cure your digger, whether he digs from boredom or because of instinct. Most dogs return to the same areas to dig (although the bored digger may change spots more often), so you will have to do a little observing. When you have identified his preferred digging area(s), thoroughly sprinkle pepper in the hole(s). (If you just fill it back up with dirt, you will find that your dog will simply dig it up again.) When he smells the pepper, he will sneeze and snort and walk away from the hole. There is also a spice named "alum" that tastes terrible and that you may use to prevent hole digging (see "Food Stealers and Trash Diggers"). *Be careful!* There is another product, called alum, which is a form of poison. Be sure to buy the alum found in the spice section in your grocery store. If it is not for human consumption, it should not be used for your pet, either.

Dogs usually dig because of boredom, but by limiting their access to certain parts of your yard, you can help to curb this behavior.

Another method I have found to be quite effective is filling the hole with dog feces. Your dog might be inclined to ignore the pepper and dig anyway, but no dog likes to get his nails and paws in feces.

The best and most logical solution for diggers that are trying to get out of the yard is to block off the base of the fence with cinder blocks, and, hello again, the garden hose! However, this means you have to watch your dog. You have to keep an eye on him, waiting for him to dig, so you can correct him. Again, if you don't like the garden hose method, have him trail a lead in the yard. The moment he begins to dig, yell "No digging!" and yank on the lead. Always give the verbal command when you administer a physical correction. It is particularly important to stop the digging behavior of the dog that is "planning an escape." He must learn to stay within the fence line. It may be a matter of his life.

For us, Nala turned into quite a backyard digger, starting first with my garden. Grrrr! I began filling holes around the yard with dog feces, but saw that she was only finding new digging spots. As annoying as this was to me, I had to spend some time watching her while she went outside. Each time she began to dig, I flung the door open, yelling, "No digging," and threw a shake can (top taped down) in her general direction. After a few days of this,

TEACHING BASIC OBEDIENCE • TRAIN THE OWNER, TRAIN THE DOG

she became suspicious that I was watching and started minding her P's and Q's. Nala is eight months old and it is now winter. While I believe she is broken of this bad behavior, I know the problem is not totally resolved. What will she do when warm weather returns and she spends more time outside? I will have to watch for this behavior in the spring and be ready to give corrections again as a reminder.

ESCAPING THE YARD

There doesn't really have to be a reason for your puppy to dig. He might be bored; he might smell something interesting in the ground; maybe he just wants to. But when your pooch escapes the yard, there is often an explanation. Before you can "fix" the problem, you should figure out what is happening.

Many unneutered males smell a female in heat and are over the fence in the blink of an eye. Many untrained, active dogs are in search of adventure. In the case of Sosi, it was anxiety.

When Nala joined our household, Sosi became quite anxious every time I left the house.

Puppies are naturally curious, and this curiosity could lead them to form an escape plan. For his safety, make sure your dog is restrained in a secure area.

Maybe she thought I was leaving her or that she was going to be replaced. Whatever the reason, any separation between Sosi and me caused her anxiety. She would escape our yard and run around to the front door, hoping to be let in that way.

The first time I realized that we had a problem was when my neighbor knocked on the door accompanied by Sosi, standing there smiling at me. I found her escape hole and blocked it off. That afternoon, another neighbor rang the doorbell. It was Sosi. I repeated the action, sure she couldn't escape this time! The next morning, I let the dogs out and stumbled back to bed. Ding Dong! Guess who? This time Sosi had hefted her chubby body over the fence. Remarkable. I was so tired I actually thought Sosi was ringing the doorbell on her own. I knew I had a problem.

I treated this behavioral problem just as I had the digging. I waited for her to escape and verbally reprimanded her. Sosi shames easily, and she was mortified. But this was not enough to resolve the problem, so I actually did four things: 1) I completely puppy-proofed the back fence. It had never been a problem before because Sosi had never done anything wrong prior to this. (She made Lassie look like a sailor on shore leave for the first time in a year.) 2) When she persisted in escaping, I located the point of escape and waited with shake can in hand. When she was in the act of climbing under the fence, I jumped out and shook the can while verbally reprimanding her. I would have to do this three or four more times before Sosi got the message to stay away from that part of the fence. (A garden hose would have been just as effective.) 3) When she entered the house by way of the back door, I praised her highly, making her feel very, very happy about coming in through the right door. 4) We had a few refresher lessons on basic obedience with long down/stays. Not only did it remind her of self-control, but the training made her feel special again. There has not been a problem since.

FOOD STEALERS AND TRASH DIGGERS

It may be a little late to mention this, but do not allow your pup to beg while you are eating, and do not allow him in the kitchen. For safety reasons alone, he should not be in the kitchen. What if he gets in your way while you are handling a boiling pot of water?

Like everything else, begging is a habit. If you occasionally give your dog food while you are eating or preparing food, he will always try. While my family eats, my dogs are in the next room. They don't even bother to beg; they know they aren't going to get any table scraps.

I have known so many dogs that are obsessed with people food. They are constantly foraging for food, begging, and yes, eventually digging into trash out of desperation. They

Bad habits, like digging in the trash, can be encouraged when you feed your dog table scraps. If you limit your dog's diet and put him on a feeding schedule, you can stop this problem behavior from occurring.

are so consumed with getting even just a little nibble that they can think of little else because *someone else is eating.*

My parent's dog has become so obsessed with food, he is actually pushy about getting something to eat. During our last visit, the girls could not sit at their little table to eat because Ziek was all over them, the plate, and the table. (My dogs know better.) My parents have to have lids on all of their garbage cans and do not dare leave out any food.

Truly, I have found that dogs that are constantly on the hunt for food are not very happy. (Not to mention that people food is not good for them.) They worry. They fret. They forage and get into trouble. Stealing food and digging in the trash is the next natural progression for them.

Just like diggers, if you have a dog who snatches people food or digs through the trash when no one is looking, you have to stay on top of him. Food will always be interesting to your dog, so you must set him up again and again. Use Bitter Apple. Make some biscuits or put out a few pieces of bread on a plate. Spray them with the Bitter Apple and set the plate out so that your pup can see it. Remember, self-correction is the best teacher. Try cookies or doughnuts the next time. Continue to set him up, using different kinds of food until he simply does not trust the food anymore.

While you are home, if you are eating pizza and watching television, set a small piece on the end of the coffee table and watch it. He can look at it, smell it and drool on it, but he is not to touch it. If he is able to resist, praise him. Again, try this one over and over again. Pretend to leave the room and watch.

To cure trash diggers, leave a tissue soaked with Bitter Apple in the trash can. When your dog takes the soaked tissue from the trash, he will drop it immediately and will experience an awful aftertaste. Do this periodically until he is no longer interested in the trash can. Try to catch him in the act, since you can't punish him if you don't (particularly if you have more than one dog). Try hiding and jumping out with a shake can while the crime is being committed.

The sooner you can break your pup of this bad habit, the better off you'll both be, and the simpler the correction process will be. However, for some people, it is not so easy. Here is an example of one such extreme method. First, I would like to warn that when you use a corrective method, it must be something you are comfortable with. Diana did not know what do to with her mixed breed that continuously dug in the trash. She even bought a trash can with a lid, but Poochie could flip up the lid and get inside. Punishing, screaming, throwing things at her pup were not working. One day, after a long day at work, Diana snapped and took up the advice of one of my colleagues. She walked in as her little friend was in the trash. Immediately, she charged Poochie, trapping her head inside the garbage can. The two struggled, while Diana wrestled pup and can over to the kitchen "everything drawer," pulled out a roll of tape, and taped the lid down over Poochie's head, trapping her head inside the garbage can. Out of breath and sweating, Diana stood back and watched as Poochie desperately banged the can around the kitchen, smacking into the fridge, the walls, and trying to escape. "I let her stay that way for a good five or ten minutes. She was trying to wrestle out and I let her stay," she said. When Poochie collapsed in a defeated heap, Diana released her. To date, Poochie shows no interest in that trash can.

I am in no way suggesting that we tape trash diggers to trash cans, just that it is only when our dogs see that we are really serious that they respond. But there is no reason for us to let the situation get so out of hand. We are supposed to be in charge. From the moment we bring our furry little friends home, we need to remind them who is the alpha male and who is the member of the pack. Maybe it really didn't occur to Poochie that she *shouldn't* be in the trash. After all, she and Diana shared a bed and food (since Diana fed Poochie table scraps). Why on earth wouldn't Diana share her trash? So often, the problems we have with our pups are actually encouraged—unwittingly—by us.

The more toys, chew bones, and bones you provide for your puppy, the less likely he will be to tear up something else. Remember, most puppies are destructive because they are

Set up situations where your dog may misbehave and try to catch him in the act. Corrections work best if you deliver them while he is committing the misbehavior.

bored or they are teething. Be sure to have dog toys that have a very hard surface. Some forms of hard rubber appear to be safe, but they can be chipped away into pieces and may make your puppy sick. Buy products that cannot be chewed up into little pieces. Remember, you are giving this toy to the puppy to distract him from other things—make sure it lasts.

When you leave the house, keep a light on if you know it will be dark before you return home. Also, the sounds of a radio or television talk show will provide comfort to your pup, and he may feel less alone. Some trainers feel that the sounds of the radio may make him feel that someone is present, which may help him refrain from chewing.

Destructive behavior can be a sign of protest. A dog may destroy something because he is angry or anxious when the owner leaves the house. Perhaps he has been left alone too much, or he just hates being left alone. I have had a lot of complaints that a dog destroyed the most recent item of clothing the owner wore. He is anxious or punishing the owner for leaving him. Attempts to gain attention do not always have to be positive. Just like children, many dogs will do anything, good or bad, to get the attention of their owners.

Once again, use "scare" techniques to discourage chewing for attention. Bitter Apple can be sprayed on the items he is chewing. If you find that he is chewing on a particular chair leg or rug, soak it with Bitter Apple. But be careful—by soaking wood with Bitter Apple you could damage the finish. Try a small area at first.

Trash diggers are more difficult to cure, but if you can remember to spray Bitter Apple in the trash cans daily, you will be able to break this habit. I have met a few dogs who actually like the taste of Bitter Apple. If this is the case, find something that he does not like; try vinegar or pepper or alum (the spice!). Still, the best correction is made when you can catch your pup in the act. Put something in the trash that smells heavenly to him. Pretend that you have left the room (or the house if you are able to spy on him), and wait. When he goes for the garbage, fly into the room and correct him.

Again, you can use the shake can method, but, if you have a puppy who is very sensitive or timid, do not use the shake can. The loud and sudden noise could make a timid dog more nervous.

Of course, many people just buy trash cans with a fastened lid or with a foot pedal. This is an effective and easy way to keep your pup out of that trash can. However, without training, you still have not taught your dog not to dig in the bathroom or bedroom trash cans.

Exercise is helpful and may be the best remedy for all problems. Long walks, nice jogs, and fun outings in the park will burn off excess energy and help your pup's disposition a great deal!

JUMPING

For larger breeds, the jumping problem is easy to solve. The best way to cure the jumper is to catch his paws *every single time* he jumps on you. In the first few seconds, it will be great fun to have you holding his paws, but hold on. Tell him "No jumping" over and over while you hold his paws. He will begin to struggle and try to pull his paws free. By holding on, you are making the jumping experience an unpleasant one for him. I promise, if you and everyone else who comes into your home grab his paws, he can be cured of this habit in less than two weeks. Some trainers have recommended stepping on the pup's back paws, but you can seriously injure his toes this way. Grabbing his front paws, verbally correcting him, and having him struggle to get away is the most effective training method. If your dog is too fast, you can also knee him in the chest (not too hard) when he jumps up. This will also cure him. I like the paw-holding method the most because it is a very gentle, yet very effective

Although most dogs jump when they are excited, even smaller dogs can cause damage or injury. Make sure you do not encourage this behavior and correct it every time it occurs.

method. If you do use the knee—do not slam your knee into your dog's chest! That is not an effective correction. Your dog should never anticipate pain from you.

For those dogs who jump everywhere and are too quick to catch, I recommend the shake can. Have one near the front door. When you come home from work or when company comes over, pick up the can as the door opens. When your pup begins to jump on or around you, shake the can and tell him, "No jumping."

Again, if you can get guests to do this, too, your pup will be cured very quickly. Children who are too small to catch the dog's paws can also use the shake can.

When it seems that your dog has been broken of this habit, set him up. Have people talk to him in an excited manner. When he gets excited, be ready to correct him. Soon he will learn to prance around people's feet. Whatever method you choose, make sure you are consistent with your corrections!

For the dog who nips, catch his muzzle in your hand and hold it. Tell him, "No," and "Bad boy." He may squeal. When he is unable to free his face from your hands it will scare him. Do not squeeze him, just hold the muzzle firmly and correct him. If you are consistent, the nipping will stop.

You definitely want to discourage any potential bad habits from the start. We tend to allow puppies to display this behavior, but we pay for it later. To allow jumping and biting in larger breeds produces obvious results. Large breeds—not realizing their strength—knock adults and children over. Smaller breeds will often jump up asking to be held. They run pantyhose, scratch legs, and may trip people when running around under their feet.

In fact, the incessant jumping of smaller dogs should be prevented if, for nothing else, their own safety and pride. Pride? Yes. Case in point: My family acquired a Poodle many years ago when my parents bought a house; the dog came with the house. It is too long a story to get into, but my strictly hound dog, mutt family was not prepared for the likes of a petite, prissy, jumping Poodle. Charlie was his name. We called him Charlie Tuna, and one day Charlie Tuna was having a particularly bad Poodle day, having just gotten a really bad haircut at the groomers. He was so humiliated when my mother picked him up that she worried about us laughing at him and further hurting his feelings. So, when my sister Michelle came home from school, my mother met her at the door and warned, "No matter what you do, don't laugh at Charlie. He's feeling very insecure." Michelle promptly burst into laughter when she saw Charlie.

Feeling guilty, Michelle greeted me at the door with the same warning. I promptly burst into laughter. Poor Charlie was a wreck. When my father got home, Michelle and I met him at the door and sternly told him not to laugh. As the "alpha male" of the house, my father's approval was particularly important to Charlie Tuna. My father is a serious man, so we felt pretty confident that he could be counted on. However, he took one look at Charlie and collapsed against the front door in laughter, dropping his briefcase to the floor.

That was the last straw for poor Charlie. He raced down the hall to find my mother. He had a habit of flinging himself into our arms when he was feeling insecure. Ready or not, jump he did. But, on this particularly bad Charlie Tuna day, he flung himself against my mother while she was brushing her teeth and ill-prepared to catch him. He bounced off her body and fell directly into the toilet. Great humiliation followed the howls of laughter.

So, you see, training is important for dogs' pride and self-esteem. My family is not alone is thinking this. Recently, when Oprah Winfrey was chosen to be on the cover of *Good Housekeeping* magazine, she excitedly told her boyfriend, Stedman, that she thought "the babies" would be on the cover with her. Her babies are two black Cocker Spaniels named Sophie and Soloman. Stedman cautiously asked, "Both dogs? Because you can't do a cover with just one." It turns out that Stedman worries about Sophie having low self-esteem and he didn't want her to feel left out.

Seriously, though, training (even just teaching a dog not to jump) helps to develop your dog's confidence and makes him a much happier and more stable dog.

If you allow your puppy to sit on the furniture while he is young, he will continue to do it when he is older. Establish household rules for your dog from the beginning and stick to them.

Jumping on Furniture

This is a very hard habit to break once it has started. If you know that you do not want your dog on the furniture, *never* let him on it from day one. People tend to let a puppy on the furniture because he is little and cute, but once he weighs over 40 pounds, it isn't cute anymore. We understand that; he doesn't.

Jumping is just like begging. For dogs who have never been allowed on furniture, they could care less and are always more comfortable on the floor or in their own bed. The alpha male does not share his furniture with his packmates—why should you? If you want to let your pup have one chair that he can sleep on, that is fine, but never let him on any other piece of furniture. Even then, you may be pushing it.

Many people resign themselves to the fact that their pets climb on the furniture during the day because the owners are not there to stop them. You may use the shake can method to stop this behavior. By this time, your pup knows about the dreaded shake can. You can leave several shake cans on the couch and the pup will not dare get near the cans. Realize, however, he may simply find another piece of furniture to lie on, unless you cover all the furniture. You can spread an expandable baby gate over your bed, for example. If you are persistent and consistent in your commands, the message will sink in.

And what about at night? It is not a particularly good idea to let your puppy sleep in bed with you. This advice has nothing to do with health or cleanliness, but is related to training. Pups, because they are pack animals, tend to consider their bed partners as littermates. It

Your dog cannot comprehend the dangers that await him outside, so make sure that he is always on leash or in a safely fenced-in area when he is outdoors.

may be easier to establish your "top dog" status if you are not the pup's bedmate. I do, however, recognize that many people like to have their dogs sleep with them. As long as there isn't a power struggle to see who is in charge, I don't really see a problem with this. But an aggressive dog should *never* be allowed on the bed or any furniture.

Children are another matter. I would especially discourage you from letting your children sleep with their dogs, even with nonaggressive pups. It is more difficult for children to establish themselves as leaders. If your pup is allowed to sleep on the same level with your child, he will regard your child as a littermate and disciplining him will be harder for the child.

BOLTING OUT THE DOOR

Obviously, this is a very dangerous problem and must be worked out quickly. During one training class, Rocky, the black Lab, bolted out of his front door and was hit by a truck. Amazingly, he was not hurt. He limped around for a day or so and was fine. Patty, Rocky's owner, asked her vet if this would cure him from running into the street again. The answer is no; you can't teach your dog to understand cars. I have known dogs who have been hit by cars three or four times. However, you can teach your dog boundaries.

I told Rocky's owners, Patty and Bill, that there were things they could do to deal with the bolting. To begin with, as they left the house for a training session, they already had the

Train your dog to wait for you before going through an open door; this way, you will be assured of his safety.

training collar and leash on Rocky. They made him do a sit/stay at the front door. Patty should have been able to slowly open the door and have Rocky stay seated until Patty told him to heel. Sometimes, when I am doing this with a dog, I will pretend to move forward. If the dog breaks his sit without being given a verbal command, he is corrected, and we try it again.

Rocky's case was a bit different. He was 10 weeks into his training and worked very well on lead. When he had the leash on, Patty could open the door and he would stay until given the command. His stays were solid enough that she could even try to trick him and he would still wait for the command to heel. His problem was that when he was off the leash, he would wait for his chance to break for freedom. There are two good training methods that can be used to solve this problem, but both require repetition and patience.

One method is to buy a long lead or light cord, approximately 15 to 30 feet, and find a sturdy place to tie one end outside the front door. Tie or fasten the other end to your pup. Bill and Patty did this with Rocky and, of course, he always thought he was going outside. So, they needed to distract him by reading the paper or cleaning near the door until he forgot about going out. Eventually, Rocky became discouraged and forgot about going out and forgot that he was wearing a leash. When enough time had elapsed, Bill or Patty would open the door from the outside and leave it open. Rocky was no dummy, so they had to pretend that one of them just came back from the store, perhaps holding something in their arms, while the door stayed open. Rocky would see his opportunity and bolt. As soon as he took off, they would call his name once. If he returned, they praised him. If he continued to run, they let him hit the end of the lead. He corrected himself.

An important point to remember when using this approach is to *be sure that you fasten the leash or cord to a flat collar. Do not do this with the chain collar.* You want your pup to get the correction of hitting the end of the lead and essentially correcting himself, but you don't want to choke him. He can really hurt his throat with the chain. Immediately call him back. When he returns, do not punish him. If you do, you will be punishing him for returning. Also, do not praise him. Simply bring him in the house and try the drill again the next day.

If you call your dog and he does not come, remember that he is tied to something. Get the lead in your hand and correct him back to you. That is, as you call him, give slight tugs on the lead, and tell him what a bad dog he is as you reel him in. Again, try this drill over and over again until he is too cautious to bolt out of the door unless you "okay" it.

A note of caution: I have had some people say that their dog picks up a lot of speed in a very short distance. If this is true of your dog, shorten the lead that you use. The longer the lead, the more speed he can get, and the greater the chances are that he will hurt himself.

A second approach to correcting bolting is to have someone outside with a shake can before you open the door. The idea is to have this person command Rocky to come back to the house when he takes off running. Bill or Patty should be the ones to do this since they have been training Rocky. Say Patty is "preoccupied" with something and opens the front door. Rocky sees his chance and bolts. Bill is waiting in the front yard. As Rocky zooms past, Bill should call to him. If Rocky shows no signs of slowing down, Bill should immediately throw the shake can and just barely miss Rocky. The sound is startling and most often, the pup will run to the owner for protection.

The moment Rocky turns back toward Bill, or even looks like he's thinking about coming back, Bill should bend over and praise Rocky. Seeing that he is not going to be punished, Rocky will run over to his owner. So often dogs are afraid that they are going to be punished and try to avoid that confrontation. The shake can acts as the bad guy and the dog is relieved to come to his owner for protection and praise. Rocky should be praised the moment he heads for Bill. You will probably have to practice the shake can method over and over again until your pup has no desire to bolt out of the house.

Also, the more you take your dog out for car rides, walks, and workouts, the better he will become. You may find that he runs out the door in excitement, but he will immediately turn around and wait for you to give him a command and/or to come out as well.

When my dogs have their collars on, they know that they must sit at the door until commanded otherwise. When I open the door wide, they stare intently at me until I make a clucking noise at them. They know we are not going to work, but they are allowed outside, and they dash outside and run around the front yard. Usually, Tasha runs a full circle, then throws herself down and stares at me, waiting to see what I am going to do next. When I ask my dogs directly if they "want to go for a car ride," once the door is open they both run directly to the car and wait. All of this came about through repetition. While Tasha was older and knew the routine, Sosi always had a leash on until she understood that she should go straight to the car or wait in the front yard. Once she completed all of her training, and I knew that she understood the different commands and routines, I allowed her to be off leash, too.

By the way, as soon as Rocky stopped limping from his run-in (literally) with the car, he went to the vet's to be neutered. That, along with his training, helped to curb his desire to bolt.

Never let your dog ride in the back of an open truck. He could fall or jump out and seriously injure himself.

CHASING CARS

Quite often, a car chaser is sitting in his front yard. He feels that the car has come too close to his territory, and he wants to chase it away. Unfortunately, each time the car speeds away, his behavior is reinforced. He believes that he has successfully chased the intruder away. There is no confrontation or lesson learned except that the car goes away, and he made it happen. The only way to stop this negative and very dangerous behavior is for your dog to learn a lesson.

The absolute best method is simply to have a friend or neighbor agree to drive in front of your house while you know your pup is outside. You should hide in the back seat of the car with a large bucket of water or a shake can. Have your friend drive by slowly enough that you will have time to react and punish your dog. As you drive past your house and he runs out to the car, lean out the window, yelling "No" and "Bad dog" and either dump the cold water on him or shake the can and throw it near his feet. This will not stop him the first few times, but each time that you do this drill, he will become more and more wary. His negative behavior is no longer being reinforced. Be sure to use different cars; otherwise, he will simply recognize the offending car and let it pass (and just think of the hours of entertainment you can provide for your neighbors!).

When you get back to the house, do not punish your dog. He may be worried about approaching you. When he comes over, love him, and act as though you have no idea what just happened. You are not the bad guy, the car is. You did not correct him, the car did. This method really works. Trust me and try it. You will be amazed, and you may save your dog's life.

BEHAVIOR PROBLEMS IN THE CAR

Rambunctious Canine Passengers

Linus Sealy was an excellent student of mine. He would heel beautifully in heavy traffic and ignore hysterical dogs who dragged their owners past us. He was just wonderful. One weekend, his owner was called away on a business meeting and I told him that I would be happy to take Linus for the weekend. He dropped Linus off at my house Friday evening.

The next morning I got ready to go to work, and I told Linus he could go with me. Everything was great until I actually started the car. It was insane. The minute I put the car into drive, he was a wild banshee. He climbed all over me, blocked my vision, and whined and whined. At one point, he actually had a paw on my chest. I was steering for dear life.

If you acclimate your dog to the car as a puppy, he will always enjoy going for rides.

There was no way to pull over or stop. When, at last, I got to a stop light, bewildered and breathless, I turned to Linus and he instantly sat down pretty as a picture and stared sweetly out the window. I was speechless! What happened? When the light turned green, he was all over me again. His paw hit my gas petal. He was everywhere at once. I could not drive, and I could not stop. Every time we got to a light, he would quietly sit down as though nothing had happened, as though he were not the hound from hell. Ha! Eventually, we arrived at work. I was so frazzled, I was shaking. I was as wild-eyed as he had been during the drive.

Much to the amusement of my coworkers, I later found out that Linus' owner also experienced the death ride, and every time he got to a stop light or anywhere he could stop, he proceeded to beat Linus until he was still. Linus, being no dummy, quickly figured out that a moving car meant there were no rules—it was every creature for himself—and stop meant be still and quiet.

The solution was to have another person drive the car while I explained the rules of life in the back seat. Rule number one: Don't put your paw in the face of the driver. Each time he began to whine or break his sit command, I would correct him and remind him of his command, "No, sit. Stay!"

Just as with walks, you should begin taking your dog for car rides as soon as you get him. Once your dog has learned basic obedience, it is neither unreasonable nor unfair to command him to sit and stay in the car. Get someone to help you.

First, have that other person drive so that you can administer the corrections. After several successful trips, have the other person sit with your pup while you drive. The rules are the same when you are behind the wheel. When he appears to be able to sit and stay, try the car ride solo—just you and your dog—but go armed with a shake can and long lead. Place the end of the lead and the shake can near you in the car. When he breaks the sit command, verbally correct him. If there is no response, grab the lead and correct him. If he becomes too rambunctious, pull over and stop the car. Once you have stopped in a safe place, give him a *firm* correction. If you are unable to pull over or cannot reach his lead when he is barking, use the shake can. Shake it and tell him, "No barking." Command him to sit. The can will usually surprise him and he will settle down, but if he does not respond, pull over as soon as possible and correct him. He has proven that he is not ready to ride alone with you in the car. Get the help of a friend again.

For those of you who have a grate or divider in your car so that your dog is confined to the back, use a 15-foot lead. Fasten it to your dog and trail the lead up to the driver's seat. When he begins to bark or jump around, pull the lead and correct him—"No! No barking!" After several corrections, you will find that he will ride quietly in the back.

After some time, he may try his luck again. Simply fasten him to the lead and retrain him. At this point, you may discover that your pup is very clever about the cause and effect relationship between barking (or doing whatever is unwanted) and being corrected. When you pull his lead, you learn that your pup's temporary quietness was because he was doing something about that relationship—chewing through the effect. You do not want him to be a lead chewer, so I recommend that you use the Bitter Apple spray and soak the lead. If he tries to chew through the lead again, he will be sorry.

At last report, Linus was able to sit still and look out the window while the car was in motion. When they came to a stop, he would occasionally peek over at his owner to see if he was going to be disciplined. He was never very comfortable with the car being stopped, but did learn to enjoy car rides like a civilized pup.

Restraining Your Dog in the Car

While you are in the car, I strongly recommend restraining your dog for your safety and that of your pet. I had a client who was in a car accident several years ago. She was strapped

Allowing your dog to roam free while you are driving can be dangerous. A crate is one way to safely restrain your dog in the car.

in, but her dog was thrown to the front of the car when their car collided with another. In this client's case, everyone was okay, but what if the owner had been knocked unconscious and the frightened dog had escaped the car and run in panic? For this reason alone, it is good to consider a seat belt made for dogs. I bought one for my sister's Dobermans, which they wear very comfortably. If you decide to purchase a seat belt for dogs, you may have to make several practice drives, that is, short drives around the block until your pup gets used to wearing it. Eventually, he will be able to wear it for longer and longer periods of time.

While I drove a Jeep in college, my Rottie, R.T., used to wear his seat belt and a pair of sunglasses. The sunglasses were for effect only, but he did look really cool wearing his seat belt! It became as second nature for him to wear it as it was for me to wear mine. Particularly in a Jeep, R.T. would never have survived a crash without wearing his seat belt.

Many people use crates in their cars or, if their cars are too small for a crate, a divider between front and back seats. Check your local pet shop.

To those people who allow their dogs to ride in the back of a pick-up truck or open vehicle, I would only say please do not do it anymore. I know he looks great with his ears

If you allow your dog to mouth or bite you when he is a puppy, it may turn into something dangerous when he matures. Stop this behavior as soon as it starts and make sure that you redirect his energy onto something positive.

flopping in the wind, but he will not look so great when he falls or jumps out. You can buy a harness that is specially designed for trucks. That way your beautiful pup will look adorable, have the fun of wind blowing his ears, and be safe, too.

MOUTHING OR SNAPPING

When our dogs are puppies, we tend to think that mouthing or snapping at our feet and hands is cute. Little fluff balls trying to act tough are amusing, and we let them growl little puppy growls. But as they get older, their little needle teeth begin to hurt and their jaws are just a bit stronger than the week before. In most cases, the snapping is in play, so we let them get away with this behavior. However, as I pointed out, the bites get a little harder and stronger each day.

In training, I see a lot of mouthing, and it is almost always very innocent. Buster, the Rottweiler, would grab a mouthful of his mistress's hair while she was trying to teach him the down command. Quite simply, he did not want to go down; he wanted to play. Lacy, the Boxer, had the same game plan in mind. While his owners busily tried to teach him stay and down, he wanted to play and would grab at their hands. Lacy continued with his mouthing for some time because his owners became very exasperated, thus making the game a lot more interesting. While they jumped around, yelled at him, wiped off slobber, and tried to correct him, he leaped around grinning hugely—Lacy-1, Parents-0.

As innocent as it appears, mouthing is a sign of dominance. Dogs do not want to listen to the command, so they grab at the hand or hair to distract the owner. A pup who is

Dogs should be exposed to children as soon as possible and should be taught to be gentle with them from the very beginning.

frustrated and does not want to learn will try to grab or snap at his owner's hands or feet, and a pup who is being punished may try to punish back by mouthing the hands.

From the moment you bring a new pup home, do not tolerate this behavior. Buster's owners began to grab his muzzle and tell him, "No mouthing," each and every time he mouthed. By doing this, they took the game away from Buster. He found out that it was not much fun to be grabbed. He tried it for about two weeks and then gave up. The key, as with everything else, is consistency. Every time your pup grabs at your hand, quickly grab his muzzle, squeeze it slightly, and tell him, "No mouthing." You can begin this method at seven or eight weeks and/or use it with adult dogs. If you are consistent, your dog will eventually learn that it is not worth the correction to mouth you.

If your dog snaps and quickly turns away, do not let this pass. Just like the car chaser, if he is not confronted, he will never learn. If he is so quick that you are unable to catch his face, and you find that in chasing him he is losing the message, have him trail a lead while you are in the house with him. The moment he snaps and tries to run away, step on the lead and reel him in. Grab his muzzle and correct him. He will not learn the first few times, but, eventually, he will learn that it just is not worth it.

If your dog actually bites you, *this is aggressive behavior.* Reread the alpha roll-over technique in the section about disciplining your dog, and consult with a trainer. This is not something to take lightly, and you may need to get professional assistance.

AGGRESSIVE BEHAVIOR WITH CHILDREN

Everyone knows how sweet Labradors are. That is why a client of mine was so upset when her Lab displayed aggressive behavior after two years of being so sweet and docile. "What has changed?" I asked. "Nothing. Well, we have a baby now," they said. Aha! There's the culprit!

Many dogs, no matter how sweet their temperaments, do not like having their position in the home threatened. Babies can seem very threatening to some dogs. Without realizing it, we tend to ignore the pup when children, especially infants, are around. In most cases, we treat the dog like a baby before the real thing comes along, and a pup cannot understand why he has been replaced. He may become very jealous of the child.

As Tramp says to Lady in the movie, *The Lady and the Tramp*, "When the baby moves in, the dog moves out." Many dogs feel this way and are understandably threatened. It is easy to feel overwhelmed by the responsibilities of a new baby, but it is essential to not forget your responsibilities as a dog owner—for everybody's sake.

Involving your child in the training process can help teach your dog to obey everyone in the family. Children also make great distractions during a training session.

While the child is napping, spend special playtime with your dog. Roll around on the floor with him, play with a toy, and give him special petting sessions. Keep up with basic obedience. It keeps him obedient, but it is also his special time, making him feel special to you. While the child is awake, include the dog in whatever activity is taking place. Show him that you can love both him and the baby. Let him sniff the baby's things and let him sleep with something that the baby smells like—a towel or little blanket, for example. Let him investigate the baby's toys and clothes, *but never leave him alone with the baby!* Never!

A dog like Sosi, who has never shown the slightest signs of aggression toward anyone, can be trusted alone with a child. I do not worry about leaving my daughter alone in a room with Sosi. For Pete's sake, this dog rounded up some baby chicks that fell from their nest and herded them into the house for me to take care of. There were three wide-eyed, squawking baby birds, streaking through the house, and Sosi looking expectantly at me, waiting for me to—I don't know, feed them or teach them to fly. But with Tasha, I did not feel the same. While Tasha is the sweetest friend, I could not take a chance that she would feel the same about babies as Sosi did. Tasha required extra reassurances that her position was not being threatened. Also, because Tasha and Sosi were already trained, I was able to walk them and the baby at the same time. And this was quality bonding time between Tasha and the baby. The baby was not a threat, but a reason for Tasha to be able to go for a walk.

Remember: Dogs don't always show signs of jealousy or aggression until it is too late. You don't want to take this chance with small children. Be watchful of any signs. If your dog is aggressive with the children, consult a professional trainer immediately. A trainer may be able to help, but you may also have to consider finding him a new home. It is unfair to your pup and your children to have an unreliable dog in the house. *It is imperative that you consult a trainer.* Sometimes dogs, like some people, just don't like small children. There is a difference between a puppy who is territorial over his possessions or feeling a little jealous, and a puppy who just plain dislikes children. A trainer can assess the situation and determine whether your pup is reliable.

Nonaggressive dogs should be exposed to children and other dogs as soon as possible. It is important that you teach your dog to be gentle with children from the beginning. Practice removing things from his mouth—toys, treats, dinner. He must learn to let go of things if you want him to. If he growls, hold his muzzle and tell him, "No" and "Bad dog." It only takes a second for a child to try to take a toy away from the wrong dog. Again, I caution you that the size of a dog has nothing to do with how protective he may feel about a toy or his food. Practice patience techniques with your dog *before* your child has the chance to provoke

Proper socialization, starting from puppyhood, will help your dog get along with other dogs. The more dogs and people he meets, the better socialized he will become.

him. Remember big Rufus, whose owners brought him for training before their baby was born? Now Rufus is a wonderful family dog.

OTHER DOGS

Socialization is so important. If your dog has been exposed to other dogs, but seems to get more aggressive as time goes on and he is a male, I would recommend that he be neutered. If your dog is aggressive with other dogs, go to a professional trainer. The trainer can work with your dog around other animals and give the proper corrections and will work with *you* as well. Do not try to work with your dog alone on an aggression problem. A trainer is experienced in handling all kinds of situations with aggressive animals. You really need to use a trainer for your safety, as well as that of your dog and others.

DEALING WITH THE AGGRESSIVE DOG

There are several categories of aggressive dogs. While training at the dog school, we had several dogs who came in by court order. We were their last stop before they would have to be put down by law.

Protective Aggressive

Prince, a Great Pyrenees, had bitten seven people. He was quiet, self-confident, and *huge.* He was a scary one because he was difficult to read. One moment he was calm and cool, willing to do a sit/stay with no protest at all, and the next moment, he would stand and slowly walk toward you—nearly 150 pounds walking menacingly toward you, daring you to make him sit again.

We will never be totally sure of the reason he bit people, except to say it was territorial. When anyone appeared "too close" to his property, be it the house or his mistress, Prince would attack. One bite, not vicious, just a stern Great Pyrenees warning to go away. Actually, he was quite majestic, but dangerous.

Had Prince belonged to one of the trainers, presumably there would never have been a first bite. But Prince had an owner who didn't fully understand or appreciate the dog he was. Truly, Mrs. T. loved her dog. Otherwise, why wouldn't she have put him down, right? But, she didn't appreciate why he did what he did. Prince, in many ways, had quietly taken over the role of alpha male in the house. It was up to him to protect, it was up to him to drive away the undesirables.

In reality, Prince should have been taught to stand back and wait for Mrs. T.'s cue. If she had indicated she was in trouble or needed his protection, then he should have come forward—not beforehand.

While I never met Prince as a puppy, I think I can safely assume he was the kind of puppy who would have protested being placed on his back. He would have kicked and clawed his way out of my grip if he could have. But he was never placed on his back, so he never learned that Mrs. T. was supposed to be in charge. While he grew, he began to find his place. Whenever Mrs. T., or anyone else in the house, tried to make him do something he didn't want to do or tried to take something away he shouldn't have, Prince would quietly, but very seriously, growl. Always a low growl, not terribly threatening to the members of the house, but they got the hint and left him alone, saying, "Geez, what a grump." In other words, he was never challenged.

As he grew into an adult, his love for the family grew. He became quite protective of them, taking the role as top dog. He was not destructive or bad in any way in the house, so he did his own thing, never causing anyone to give him a correction. Now, suddenly, I was looking at a large dog who, in all honestly, was toying with me. I amused him because I was gently trying to test him. Basically a good-natured dog, he didn't want to hurt me. In fact, he liked me. I took him places, petted him, and told him how handsome he was. But, he watched me. I was pushing the borders. We both knew it.

Training with him went slowly. There were two different tactics I could use. Head on, aggressive, forced confrontation, which is effective and would have worked—eventually. Or there was a gradual training process, building a respect for each other. Always, I was prepared to do battle if he resisted a command, but by moving more slowly, he worked through commands. He ate lunch with me, we talked about things while he sat in a sit/stay. Slowly, while he went into down/stays, I rubbed his belly, turning him over. While I leaned over him, scratching his belly, I stood over him, giving gentle commands like, "Stay. Good boy. Good stay."

As our respect was building, I asked more and more of him. He began to do what is so natural of his breed, of all dogs—he wanted to please me. We made this transition from trainer to owner. Prince loved his people, but *pleasing* them wasn't really a priority. Protecting them was.

High collaring was very important for Mrs. T. to learn. While they were out walking, Mrs. T. had to high collar Prince when new people came around, telling him to stay over and over again.

Mrs. T. will always have to watch Prince when he is around strangers. This is a fact. However, by changing the string of command, so to speak, Prince's owners were able to change his aggressive/protective behavior. This meant things had to change in the house. Prince was not allowed on furniture. If he grumbled a challenge at someone, very casually the person would walk over to him and immediately put him in a down/stay, turning him over on his back so they could stand above him. As simple as this sounds, rolling him over and making him stay became the very thing that saved his life and made him more compatible with his family.

Shy/Sharp Aggressive

Wolfenstien came to us also as a last resort. In the home, he was extremely affectionate. In fact, unlike Prince, Wolfenstien's owners could do anything to him. They could roll him over or mouth his neck if they wanted to. (They didn't.) He was a regular pussycat in the home with his people.

Outside the immediate family, it was a different story. Wolfenstien didn't trust anyone and was terrified of the world. Instead of submissive wetting, Wolfie attacked. He had bitten several of the children's friends and lunged wildly at anyone who came near. Part Boxer and who-knows-what-else, he was adopted at an older age. His background was unknown. From

Some dogs can use their protective instincts to participate in sports like Schutzhund or police work, but these exercises only should be undertaken by someone who is properly trained and has had experience handling aggressive dogs.

the age of ten months, when he was adopted into his new family, he was already terrified of the world. Shy/sharp animals almost always bite out of fear, when they feel backed against a wall. Shy/sharp aggressive animals may actually chase someone but, again, it is in fear. Not very comforting if you're the guy being chased on top of a car, but that is what a shy/sharp aggressive animal is—fearful. It is safe to say that Wolfie never had any socialization as a puppy. This is why trips to the park, riding in the car, walking outside of your neighborhood, meeting other dogs and people, and being placed in unusual situations are so good for young dogs. If they are exposed to all of this as a puppies, they are almost always more even-tempered as adults.

Wolfenstien was actually more dangerous than Prince. Prince only bit when someone threatened his owners in some way. Coming too close and body contact were seen as threats to Prince and his family. But Wolfenstien had no boundary guidelines. He lunged at, chased, and attacked anyone he saw. There was no age, sex, or size discrimination.

Training Wolfie was very similar to training Prince, except we had to start with a muzzle. It wasn't something either one of us particularly enjoyed, but it was necessary. The first two days, he spent all his time trying to bite my left knee. Even though I knew he could not hurt me, it was a bit disconcerting to have this ferocious growling and snapping at my left side, as he shoved his face against my leg. I could feel his hot breath against my leg.

Trust was the successful factor with Wolfie. On the third day, I removed the muzzle, keeping the chain high collared around his neck. With my elbows raised high and bowed out, I was ready for him to lunge at me. Having my arms readied in this manner I would be able to immediately jerk up, holding him away from me. He was a rather large dog, and I would not have been able to keep him up for long, but I knew it would save me from the initial attack. If needed, I would be able to jerk the lead around, keeping Wolfie off-balance. Eventually, I would win, pinning him down on the ground. If needed, he would go on what trainers call "a helicopter ride." It's not something I like to do, and not anything I will teach in this book. If your own dog is so aggressive with you that a helicopter ride is needed, you need to seek a professional immediately!

Fortunately, none of this was needed. As it turned out, Wolfie watched me closely, but he never lunged. He never growled. He never bit. He just watched me very closely. I moved slowly, I told him everything I wanted beforehand and spoke gently. When he obeyed, I praised him so much that I thought he might wiggle his little Boxer nub off. What he was seeking, as all pups do, was to make me happy. Once he realized I was not going to hurt him, but actually loved him, he loved coming to school.

On the first day of school it had taken three trainers to get him into his stall and safely secure him without anyone being bitten. By the second week, I was spending my lunch hour in his stall with him, leaning against the wall, sitting side by side, sharing lunch with him. He even had a sense of humor, thinking it was funny to smack his water bowl once I was sitting down so I would get my pants wet. He thought this was very funny.

Wolfie remains one of my most joyous training memories and one of my greatest reality shocks. You see, when he left school he was heeling, sitting, performing down and out-of-sight stays on the 15-foot lead with no problems. His recalls were beautiful. Our bond was based on trust and mutual respect. He had all the elements of becoming a sound, stable, happy pup. Once he went home, however, his owners did not keep up with the lessons. A Labrador Retriever can go weeks or months without a training session and quickly remember as soon as one begins again. Wolfie needed daily training and constant reinforcement because he was so fearful He needed the daily confidence-building regimens of basic obedience. Wolfie was a high-maintenance pup most people would not want to deal with.

For a brief period, when I saw how happy and pleased his people were, I thought he had a chance. But Wolfie was eventually put to sleep. Within three weeks he was back to his same nervous routine. They had not continued the training and without it, Wolfie was hopeless. It was a very unfortunate and unhappy event. It was some time before I shared my lunch with any furry people in their stalls.

Another example of shy/sharp behavior is Cody, the Airedale. Remember he was put on a shock collar for faster results? While his people were out of town, Cody stayed with me. Of course, I didn't let the shock collar anywhere near my house, but the damage was already done.

One Saturday morning my family was in the bedroom. My husband, my children, and all of the dogs were there. My eldest daughter said she wanted to pet Cody, so she slid off one side of the bed and went toward Cody, sitting alone in the corner. Without warning, he lashed out. I was not present when this happened, but by the description my husband gave, I knew what had happened. I confirmed my feeling with several other trainers as well as animal behaviorists from Ohio State University. Cody, we all agreed, was an abused dog.

To the defense of his owners, they had no idea they were part of this abuse. They had been skeptical about the shock collar at first, but the "professional trainer" had convinced them this was the way to go. What they could not know was when I first called the other professionals for second opinions, each and every person guessed the name of the trainer responsible for this. Other professionals were familiar with his "work" since they often had to try to undo the damage.

Throughout this book, I have suggested you contact a trainer for more diffiuclt problems, but be wary! Call the Better Business Bureau, the Society for the Prevention of Cruelty to Animals, and local veterinarians for references.

In Cody's case, he did not begin life as a shy/sharp dog, but as a result of poor training methods he became one. He became shy/sharp as a result of the shock collar. When Kerri closed in, Cody became agitated and struck out to protect himself. Unlike the story of Wolfenstein, this one has a happy ending. Cody's people are through with the shock collar and have begun the slow, reliable, happy way of training with Cody, and Cody is a much happier, more reliable dog.

Aggressive or Not?

I hear a lot of people say their dog isn't aggressive, but he will go after other dogs. If your dog attacks other dogs, chases after kids, bites, challenges members of the family over a piece of furniture or a spot on the bed, or growls when you come too close to his dog dish, he is displaying signs of aggression or aggressive *tendencies*. This must be dealt with.

I had a 10-year-old Dalmatian client that was very aggressive with other dogs. I could have laid on top of him and bitten his toenails if I wanted—I didn't. He could not have cared less. But if he saw a small dog down the street, he wanted blood. His owners worried he was too old to learn. Nonsense. No matter what the age of your pup, he must be taught what is acceptable behavior and what is not. In the wolf pack, any wolf who gets out of line is immediately "notified" by the top dog. That would be you.

Any time there is a display of aggressive behavior, you must react. Remember the alpha male roll-over? You must do it quickly and effectively.

I will give you an example of reacting immediately. Last week I was working with an aggressive Doberman. He is fine with other dogs and adults. But he is unpredictable with kids. He just does not like them. So, as we were passing two young girls, I high collared JoJo. With fists one on top of the other clenching the leash, I was ready. There was no slack in his lead as I held it up over his head, keeping the collar high behind his jawline. If he tried anything, I would be right there. And, as it turned out, he did. At the last moment, as the little girls were almost past us, he lunged out sideways trying to grab hold of the child's coat.

There were a lot of people around and what he did was very surprising. The two worst things I could have done would be to be embarrassed and not correct JoJo as he needed because there were a lot of people watching or to begin apologizing profusely to the child. JoJo needed immediate reprimand for what he did. "No!" I shouted, jerking him hard several times. "No! No! No!" Then, I commanded that he go down. Not really waiting for his typically slow response to the down command (and that is a sign of dominance when a dog reacts very slowly to the down command), I pushed him down, quickly stepping on the lead where the clasp was. By stepping on the lead at the very top, you help pin the dog down. Be careful: Be sure that your shoe does not unclasp the leash from his collar. Step on the clasp so that it is flat on its side.

Once JoJo was down, I instantly rolled him over and leaned over him, all the while telling him what a wretched little beast he was. My voice was very stern. I gave him one final glare. Once I knew he was not going to move or challenge me, and when he looked very remorseful, I looked back at the child. Always address the dog first. For one thing, the dog

Your dog must know that you are the leader of his pack and look to you for discipline and guidance.

has to be controlled so that he cannot try to bite the child again. If JoJo was going to learn from this, he must be reprimanded immediately. Fortunately, the child was unharmed, but had she been bitten, it would have been imperative for me to put JoJo down all the same, making sure he didn't try to bite her again.

Now, if JoJo had fought me, I would have had to wrestle him down in front of an audience. I have seen this many times and I can assure you that in the canine world, challenging a top dog is unheard of. If your pup challenges you and refuses to be rolled over, he doesn't take you seriously in your role as top dog.

If you need to do an emergency down/roll-over and your pup fights you, toss all dignity out the window. If you do it right the first time, chances are good there won't be a second time.

The first thing to do is get the top of the lead under your foot. As you step down on the lead, the weight of your body will force his head down to the sidewalk. If he is still standing but his head is being pulled down by the collar and your weight, then pushing on his shoulders will easily force him down.

While I was visiting in her home, Roxie, the Wonder Beagle, growled at her owner when she was shoved from the couch. Mrs. W. scowled at Roxie and said, "Stop that," to show her

Allowing your dog on your furniture or in your bed can confuse the issue of who is "top dog" in your household.

disapproval. Guess how much impact that had on Roxie? If you guessed zero, you are only half right. What happened was that Roxie took a stand, displaying her dominance, and no one called her on it. Not only did she get away with unacceptable behavior (challenging her top dog), but now she thinks she is pretty hot stuff and is actually making plans to turn Mrs. W.'s home into the Animal Farm. For a dog like Roxie, a dog with aggressive tendencies, *not* correcting unacceptable behavior *creates* an aggressive dog down the line. I hope this is clear: People actually encourage dogs to become aggressive by not correcting them properly. Roxie, like JoJo and so many others, was merely testing her boundaries. How far will she go? Growling at you is just the first step.

While this scenario never happened because I was just visiting Roxie and Mrs. W. in their home, I fantasized about what might have been, what should have been. Imagine this. There I was, sitting on the couch when Roxy came up to greet me.

Commercial interruption: I understand that allowing dogs on the furniture is a personal preference. I must say, because I am a good dog trainer, your dogs should not be allowed on your furniture. There should be an understanding in your relationship about who gets furniture and who doesn't. Allowing dogs on the furniture really confuses the top dog issue and is actually, as odd as this might sound, unfair to the dog. Now, having said that, we may continue with this fantasy. . . .

After some time, I push Roxie to the side and she growls. "What?" I say, taking hold of her collar and forcing her down to the floor. Once she is on the floor I say, "I don't think so.

You don't growl at me. No. Bad girl. No. Down!" I continue to tell her, "Down," physically making her go down, and repeat how bad she is for growling at me. She won't understand the exact words, but Roxie is no dummy. She screwed up on that one, and she will know it. "Down. Stay!" Leaning over her, I make her lie down and stay under my watchful, top-dog-like gaze.

If done properly, Roxie will draw her little paws up, looking half nervous and half sorry. I make her stay there for two minutes. Although my voice softens a bit, I still mutter, "I can't believe you did that. You know better than that. You don't growl at me, little lady." She hears my voice of discontent. Two minutes are up and I say, "Okay, you can get up. Okay." I do not allow her back up on the couch to say "Sorry."

Even if you allow your pup on furniture (ahem), definitely do not allow him right back up to the scene of the crime. If he tries to fight you on the down command, or he goes down but then tries to slink away, you must react. Again, if you ignore this, there is no point to the initial correction. You must see the process through. If he fights the down, wrestle him down! Show him who is boss and physically keep him down for those two minutes. If he goes down but then tries to sneak away, stop him, hold him, and repeatedly tell him to stay.

In-home training is so important. We want our pups to behave themselves on leash when we are in public, but we let them behave like little loons in the house. In their minds, it does not work that easily. They must have consistency. There must be rules in the house and out of the house. Dogs really do want guidance, just as children do.

For those who have the ongoing battle over who is actually in charge, long down/stays in the house are a must. If you have a dog who has growled at you, you are being challenged.

CORRECTING AGGRESSIVE BEHAVIOR

Obviously, burying your face into that of an aggressive animal is not a wise decision. Not only is the eye contact incredibly threatening to the animal, often making him more aggressive, but it is also potentially dangerous for the handler. The following is another effective way to correct bad behavior.

Alpha Roll-Over

This method of correction should be used only when your dog has committed a capital offense. Examples of this would be snapping or growling at you or other people or aggressive behavior with other animals after repeated correction. The alpha roll-over is a type of discipline that has been used mainly for extremely aggressive or dominant dogs.

You can discipline your dog for a serious offense by performing the alpha roll-over; quickly roll your dog over onto his back and force him to submit to you. This is the way in which the leader of the pack establishes authority.

If you observe wolf pack behavior, you will see that the leader of the pack will, from time to time, "take down" a member of the pack who challenges his authority. It is important that you do this to establish yourself as leader—and do it quickly. This is very similar to, but more severe than, the roll-over discussed earlier. In the section "Which Puppy in the Litter," the roll-over technique is used to determine the pup's personality; the technique in this section is to be administered as a correction.

First, have the dog immediately sit, then lie down. If he does not know how to go down or fights the command, once he is in a seated position, lean forward and grab one front leg (the one opposite you). While you pull the leg with one hand, gently but firmly push the dog's body down with your other hand.

Once the dog is down, roll him over onto his back. Do not be gentle. This is part of the discipline. Your dog instinctively knows what is happening. He may submit immediately by exposing his neck and turning his eyes away so as not to look at you. At this point, you are the dominant one; he has acknowledged this with his behavior. However, it is not always so easy. Your dog may attempt to challenge you. He will fight, refusing to roll over on his back.

When this happens, quickly straddle the dog so that your body can hold him in place, and use your free hands to perform the shake down method. That is, grab his jowls and pull his face upward. Using familiar commands, such as, "No! Bad boy," make eye contact until he yields and looks away. This is a way in which the leader of the pack establishes unquestioned authority without causing physical damage to another member of the pack.

Your dog should relax and stop the fight. The final step will be when he turns his head to avoid eye contact and exposes his neck. The more submissive animal may remain in this position for some time after the shake down. A more dominant, aggressive dog may put up more of a struggle, but do not let him win. Remember, you have to be "top dog" in the end.

My friend Sara's ten-month-old Dobie, JoJo, has been vying for the top dog position for some time. For this reason, I have been warning that he should not be allowed to sleep in bed with her. When Sara, Jenny (a five-year-old Shar-Pei), and JoJo sleep together, JoJo thinks of this as his pack. There are no leaders in this pack, because they are all on the same level. While this setup would not be a problem for most dogs, JoJo is much more dominant. He is the typical alpha male. He is aggressive, dominant, and "in training" to rule the pack. At the tender age of ten months, he has growled at several people who are in his pack. Sara

---

Rolling over and exposing his stomach not only puts your dog in a submissive position, it allows him to enjoy an affectionate tummy rub.

is one of them. JoJo has never so much as entertained the idea of growling at me because we have a much different relationship. He knows I am the leader, that I am top dog. To challenge me would surely bring him misery—at least, that is how he sees it and that's fine by me.

It was no surprise when I got a phone call one morning from Sara. JoJo had growled at her when she tried to move him over in the bed. I was pleased to hear that she immediately put him in the alpha roll position. But he should never have been in the bed in the first place. This is not to say that Sara can never enjoy sleeping with her dogs, but until this behavior is straightened out, he cannot have the sense of being equal in the pack. JoJo is the perfect example of why training is so important for both owner and pup. While he is learning proper behavior, Sara is learning the rules of the canine world. They will grow together and develop a much stronger, healthier relationship.

Whatever method of correction you choose, adhere to one rule: Never call your puppy to get his "punishment." Go to him and bring him to the mistake. Do not teach him that by coming to you he may be punished. There is a part two to this rule. When your dog has made a mistake, do not make eye contact with him as you are approaching him. This is because he may look and run before you have a chance to collar him. A five-minute chase scene will mean he has forgotten what he has done to deserve punishment.

We have talked a lot about aggressive dogs, why they are aggressive, and how to handle them, but there is one more serious issue that must be addressed. Many dogs become problems because we, the owners, create them. I cannot tell you how many clients I have had who enjoy the tough-guy images of their dogs. They like having dogs that are feared or should be feared. I don't understand this. What is the point? Some people may answer that they got their dogs for protection, rather than companionship. To this, I say that dogs have been faithful and fearless companions to humans, protecting our territories for tens of thousands of years. You don't have to make your dog antisocial to do what comes naturally to him anyway.

I know a woman who had Bulldogs for much of her adult life. She enjoyed the fact that some of them were fiercely territorial and tells proudly of how one Bull chased a salesman up a telephone pole. As an older woman, she was given a Sheltie. Shelties are smaller and more manageable than Bulls. But not so with Beau. By the time Ms. W. was through "training" Beau, he was a thoroughly unenjoyable dog. He barked constantly and was always on alert. He charged other dogs and snapped at people. It got to the point where she could not manage or walk him. Everyone, Beau included, was miserable. Shelties are wonderfully fun, high-spirited dogs to be with, but Ms. W. completely changed his personality so that no one wanted to be around him.

Remember Levi, the Pit Bull? His owner's greatest concern was not that Levi learn his basic obedience and be a great addition to the family, but that he was not going to be aggressive enough.

Remember when Sosi, the wonder, chicken-herded a gaggle of baby birds into my house? This same dog, the dog that is afraid of cats, charged a maintenance man who walked unannounced into our house. At first, we thought it was Tasha. As we ran down the hallway toward the barking, we discovered that Sosi was barking ferociously at the man while Tasha stood back watching. When it came down to it, the very dog who could be run out of town by Morris the Cat made a stand and guarded her home and people against a "highly dangerous" plumber.

Our dogs, by nature, will protect us when necessary. There are too many stories to count about the heroism of dogs. But we, as dog owners, have a responsibility to our dogs and, to our human neighbors, to let the true wonderful natures of canines develop on their own. We have a responsibility to continue to nurture the very positive relationship that has gone on for so long between humans and dogs. We also have a responsibility to make sure our dogs are stable members of our families and society, not menaces shaped by misguided machismo.

HOW TO HANDLE A STRANGE, AGGRESSIVE DOG

As unpleasant as this subject is, you should teach your child how to react to a dog attack.

• If a dog charges you while you are riding a bike, do not try to outpedal him. Stop and quickly get off the bike, placing the bike between you and the dog. Do not make eye contact. Slowly back away, always keeping the bike between you and the dog.

• If you are walking or jogging and a dog suddenly runs up to you, stand still. Do not run away. *Do not scream.* Running and screaming will only excite the dog more. In a deep, loud voice, tell the dog to go away. As you do this, back away. Once you are out of the dog's territory, he will go away.

• If you are actually attacked by a dog or dogs, drop to the ground and curl into a ball, placing your arms and hands over your head. This will protect your head and neck, and give you the most protection against bites. Kicking and screaming will only excite the dog(s) that much more. Assuming the position of a submissive animal may be the only thing to save you until help arrives.

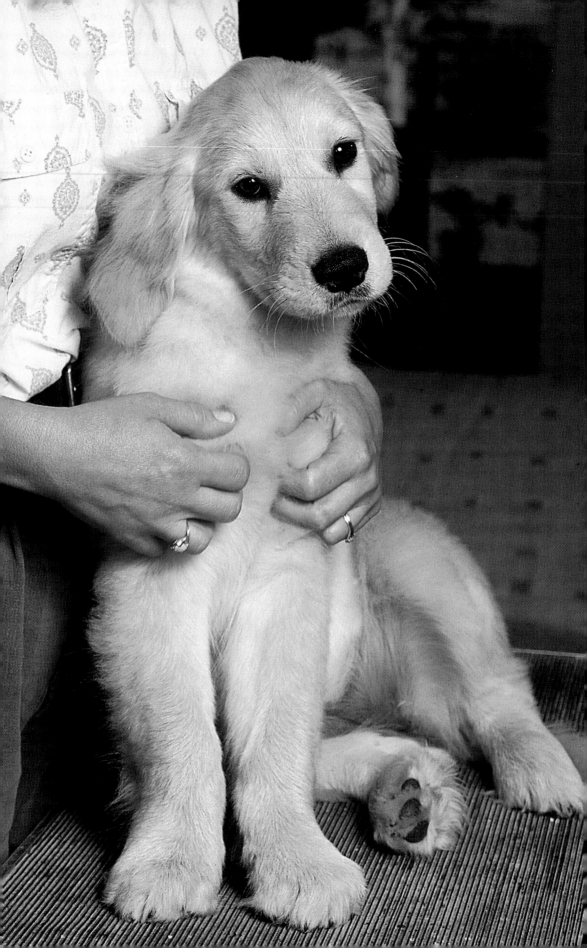

Part Four

LOVING TOUCHES

PREPARING FOR THE YEARS TO COME

SOCIALIZATION AND FEARS

I'm taking my eldest daughter to day care because I am afraid she thinks she is a puppy. I have stayed home to raise my children because I thought, at home, they would receive the very best of care. However, of late, I have noticed that my toddler eats dog kibble, makes woofing noises, and insists on eating her cereal out of her bowl on the floor like a puppy. When she is ready for her nap, she drags her beloved pillow over to the dogs' beds and plops down. Her favorite toys are balls and squeaky toys.

Last week when I caught her licking water out of the dog bowl, I knew something had to be done. I thought I was doing so well, but I realized I've been making one of the most common dog owner errors. My daughter is in dire need of socialization. So, after picking her up from her first day at day care, I was not surprised to learn that she "does not play well with others."

Socialization is as important for dogs as it is for people. It is vital to you and your pup that you take him out as often as possible. It is one of the key tools to having a happy, healthy dog you can enjoy. All too frequently, I am asked to train dogs who are terrified of traffic, the sounds of trucks, people, or other animals. In almost every case, I need not ask the history of the puppy—I already know. He has spent most of his life in his backyard and/or house. The only time he rides in the car is to go to the vet. The result is always the same. This kind of isolation creates unpredictable dogs who are unable to handle any situation that is different from their normal home life.

A well-socialized dog is one who can walk calmly near traffic, behave around other dogs, and sit quietly in a car. This is an animal that can be taken to picnics, parades, long walks in the park, anywhere. Unfortunately, dog owners don't think of this until that special occasion is upon them.

The Big Wide World

Basil, an eight-month-old male Newfoundland, spent most of his life in his two-story home and big backyard. He had been to the vet's a dozen or so times, and occasionally went in the family car to drop the kids off at school. Other than that, he knew only his yard and house. Only when a company picnic turned disastrous—Mr. C. still won't talk about it, but I know it had something to do with the boss and a paper plate full of baked beans—did Basil come to school and a whole new world opened up for him. With Basil, we rapidly went through the standard paces: heel, sit, down, stay, and come. Basic obedience was not a

It's a big wide world out there, and you and your dog should take the journey together. Introducing him to as many different situations and people as possible will make him a well-rounded and well-socialized pet.

problem for Basil. Outside, Basil would go through the paces beautifully. But the black-and-white tiles inside the store made him a wreck. He seemed to believe that the floor was going to swallow him whole. It took many torturous (for him) lessons in the store before he relaxed and realized the floor wasn't going to eat him.

Chaka, a two-year-old male Rhodesian Ridgeback, had never seen ceiling fans before and cowered to the floor, having to be dragged across it. Chaka had been a star student, but upon seeing a ceiling fan he was a wreck. His owner and I found a store that would allow us to come in, and we practiced walking through the store over and over again. I was the ogre of the shopping mall strip, dragging a pathetic, helpless dog across the floor while he peered up fearfully at the ceiling.

With Boris, a 210-pound Mastiff, stairs were the jaws of death. I could see this training was not going to be pretty. The process involved dragging him up and down the stairs until he could comfortably walk them himself. It was difficult, but possible. Once he started to get the hang of it, woe to anyone else on the staircase. I can still hear the piercing screams of Karen, another trainer, as she was dragged down the stairs by a speeding Boris, bouncing

---

Dogs can suffer from fears and insecurities, just as people do. Kinder, a Doberman Pinscher, sucks on her pillow when she becomes nervous.

like a ragdoll. When it had become clear to Boris that Karen was going to make him take the stairs, he decided the only way to do it was to get it over with as quickly as possible, running as fast as his powerful legs would carry him. This would not have been so scary with a Cocker Spaniel or even a medium-sized Labrador, but 210 pounds is a lot of dog to stop. Loud stomping, cursing, and dragging sounds could be heard outside the building. But we repeated the process of climbing up and down the stairs over and over and over until Boris felt confident to go up and down without being terrified and without injuring anyone. Practice makes perfect (or close to it).

My sister's dog, Kinder, sucks on her pillow. When she is feeling insecure and she can't find a pillow, a quilt or blanket will do. While visiting us, Kinder became nervous with all the toddler activity in the house. (Can't say that I blame her. If I thought it would help, I would suck on a pillow, too.) But, alas, as I have tried to explain to Kinder, it doesn't make things better.

While it looks very cute to have your puppy sucking on a pillow, there are problems. First, the sucking is almost enabling, allowing Kinder to draw into her timid little hole. Gently remove the pillow or blanket from your pup's mouth and engage him in play or performing a trick. This will help build his confidence.

The second problem is that the sucking can turn destructive. After a while, sucking may not be enough, and your dog may begin tearing at the cloth. The best long-term plan is to encourage your dog to become part of the group instead and feel comfortable enough that he does not need to pacify himself on something.

Training and confidence are the keys.

Thunderstorms and Firecrackers

Many dogs are frightened by loud booming noises and may cringe and shiver during a thunderstorm. The worst thing you can do for your dog is hug him and try to soothe his fears. This sounds hard-nosed, I know, but it will only make his fears worse. If you ignore the noises and act as though you do not notice anything unusual, it will minimize his fears. If you don't notice it, maybe it's not so bad.

To deal with this problem effectively, put your pup in his crate or a small, windowless room—like a center bathroom or closet—with a favorite toy during a storm or, for example, on the Fourth of July. He will feel more secure in there. Once the storm or celebration is over, act as though nothing happened. (If you have an outdoor dog, please be sure he has adequate shelter. See the section entitled "Climate Considerations.")

Confronting Fears

Whatever their socialization problems, each of my students had to confront his fears to be able to continue training. As long as the situation was safe, we tackled the fear. Whether I was doing long down/stays on the tile floor with Basil, sitting at the entrance way of the ceiling-fanned store with Chaka in my lap, or walking up and down the stairs 456 times with Boris, these pups had to slowly, carefully work through their fears so that they would be reliable with their owners.

My fear has always been this: a repeat of Kiki, a beautiful Okbosh (a rare Turkish sheep herding breed). The owners wanted this very expensive pup to be off-leash trained and laid down an extra large bonus to do so. My evaluation determined that Kiki was a bit skittish. I wasn't comfortable with the idea of off-leash training, but was overruled. Working on a 6-foot or 15-foot lead, she was perfection. Eager to please, my wish was her command. She would sit quietly while dogs, cats, and squirrels paraded past her. Passersby would marvel at her beauty, bend over and hug and pat her; she would never budge. Nothing could break her stay, until a bus came by. Then, she was gone like a shot. It wasn't that she disobeyed me;

A training class will not only help teach your dog basic obedience, it also can be a great place to socialize with people and other dogs.

she didn't even hear me. The buses were so terrifying to her, she lost control of herself and fled. Picture this; five trainers weaving through traffic, trying desperately to catch this dog before she ran into the heavy traffic on the main street, one block away. If she got there, she would never escape unharmed.

As Kiki slipped past another trainer, she had only me to dodge before she was home free and on the busy street. It's strange how animals who panic about traffic rush straight to it, as if in a trance. She had *that* look. In a frantic last-gasp effort, I did a dive tackle that would later earn me a round of applause and the nickname "Randy Macho Man Savage" from my fellow trainers. Kiki and I rolled over and over one another and came to a stop just short of the busy boulevard.

When Kiki's owners came to pick her up, they were told they would find Kiki and me on the busy street, watching traffic and "having a talk." We did talk, too. We talked about how dangerous it was to run away and how it was going to be a very long summer. Kiki was not going to do any more off-leash training for some time, and she spent a lot of time with me.

The unpredictability of unknown fears or aggression is the reason I work dogs in so many different environments—in empty parking lots; near traffic and buses; near schools; in parks, with grass and children and dogs and squirrels. I work my dogs in all these scenarios before I even consider off-leash training. You may train your pup with the neighborhood cat sauntering around as a distraction. Perhaps your pup does everything perfectly, learning to ignore the cat. Yet, when he is off leash, he may take off after another cat or squirrel that runs away from him. There is a big difference between a sauntering cat and a fleeing cat. Remember, a dog's instinct tells him to chase fleeing cats and squirrels. You have to train him otherwise and prepare him (and you) for every possible scenario before you can know he is reliable.

Socialization, which never really seems that important until it's too late, can truly save the life of a dog. It can help prevent treacherous and exhausting car rides, avoid dog fights, and allow you and your dog to walk comfortably along crowded sidewalks. Socialization will also prevent your pup from greeting guests by jumping on them and knocking them over, mouthing them and slobbering on silk blouses.

OBESITY

Obesity is the most common nutritional disease in dogs and is associated with many health problems. Studies show that more than 25 percent, and perhaps as many as 44 percent, of American dogs are obese. Besides shortening the life span of your pet, obesity causes joint and locomotion problems such as arthritis, spinal disc problems, and damaged ligaments; breathing difficulties; heart disease; high blood pressure; liver disease; diabetes; and gastrointestinal problems, including pancreatitis, ulcers, and constipation. Obesity causes overall discomfort for your dog and can result in heat intolerance and irritability. In addition, obesity can be a critical health problem for older dogs, as I will discuss a little later.

Obesity is caused, in most cases, by the dog consuming too many calories for his energy needs—that is, too many calories and not enough exercise. Overfeeding puppies predisposes them to obesity as adults by increasing the number of fat cells in their bodies. A fat puppy will be hampered with a weight problem throughout most of his life.

You can determine if your pup's weight is normal by performing a simple test. Feel his rib cage. If you can feel the ribs, then he is fine. If the ribs are difficult to feel, he is overweight. If you cannot feel the ribs at all, he is obese. *Put him on a diet.* Be sure to talk to your vet about how much your dog should now eat; you don't want to starve him or deprive him of nutritional needs. Also, verify with your vet that your dog is healthy and that his weight is not a sign of another problem, such as heart or kidney disease. Your vet will help you determine a proper diet for your dog and a reasonable time frame for weight loss, if it is needed. You should also consult your vet about introducing exercise into your dog's life again. Even a walk around the block is exercise for an otherwise sedentary dog. Remember, you can make your dog's life happier, healthier, and longer.

FEEDING YOUR DOG AND SPECIAL DIETS

During the years I have trained, I have had a houseful of dogs. Needless to say, costs of dog food can be tremendous. When I first got into training, I looked for cheap deals on 20-pound bags of food. It did not take me long to figure out that the food was going right through the dogs and into the backyard.

As I learned more about nutrition and the different foods on the market, one thing became clear. If you feed your dog junk, you are cheating him of a proper diet, and you are going to spend a lot of time with your pooper scooper. A lot of foods on the market are made of fillers—cheap cereal that offers little or no nutritional value. You get what you pay for. My best advice: Consult your vet and local pet store owners to find out about nutritious brands of food. If you decide to buy the cereal foods found in the grocery stores, you can add supplements yourself to create a more substantial diet. Add one tablespoon of kelp, one teaspoon of brewer's yeast, and a dash of vegetable oil, and mix into his bowl of food.

You should choose a dog food that is nutritious and formulated for your dog's stage of life and level of activity.

Feeding your dog only steak is just as bad as feeding him cheap cereal foods. Steak, or any meat, is an unbalanced diet. I had a client named Gretchen, a Dachshund, whose masters owned a restaurant. They were proud to say that she ate only the best—steak. But, by the time Gretchen was four, she had teeth problems and a poor coat. These are frequently the results of this kind of diet.

I have often seen poor diets in the more petite breeds. Their owners tend to feel that their little mouths are too sensitive for hard foods. This is not true. Soft foods and unbalanced diets are the most harmful.

This brings me to the subject of people food. Too many owners feed their dogs people food, and these foods tend to be particularly bad for dogs. Chocolate and the skin of turkey can be lethal for dogs. Pork chop bones easily splinter and can cause intestinal damage. Yet, we feed these things to our dogs thinking of them as treats or something the dog needs. Talk with your vet about what you feed your dog. I know two dogs who are obese, although their owner claims that she feeds them just one cup of food a night. What she does not mention is the milk, pizza, and yogurt-covered pretzels she shares with them. Of course, your dog loves these treats but, in the long run, feeding them to him will ruin his health.

Treats can be a great reward when your dog performs well; just make sure that they are nutritious and do not upset his regular diet.

Good Pup Treats

You can make healthy treats for your pup at home. This way you can avoid the artificial colors and dyes that are put in commercial dog treats.

Here is a list of ingredients:

5 cups of wheat flour

2 cups of boiling water

1 cup of dry milk

3/4 cup of butter

4 beef bouillon cubes

2 eggs

Dissolve the beef bouillon cubes in the hot water and combine all the ingredients. Roll into 1/4- or 1/2-inch thick pieces or use a cookie cutter. Bake at 350 degrees until hard, usually 20 minutes.

If you are baking for a smaller dog, you may reduce all the measurements by half. I have tried both chicken and beef flavorings. My dogs love both, but the beef is their favorite.

Tasha Treats

The ingredients are:

1/3 cup of water

3 tablespoons of oil

1 cup of wheat flour

1/4 cup of soy flour

Mix the ingredients together and use a cookie cutter or press dough flat on a cookie sheet. Bake at 350 degrees until brown, usually 12 minutes.

Special Diet Needs

If your dog has been diagnosed with a kidney problem or he requires a low-sodium diet, your vet can recommend a specialized food for your pet. However, these specialized foods can be costly. You can easily make a food specialized for your dog's needs.

This recipe is an example:

1 lb of ground beef

1/2 cup of corn meal

1 cup of rice

1/2 cup of oatmeal

1 tablespoon of barley

3 tablespoons of garlic powder

Mix corn meal, oatmeal, and rice in boiling water until thickened. Add a dash of garlic powder and barley for flavoring. In a separate skillet, brown the ground meat until it is well cooked. Drain *all* the grease. Mix the ground beef into the other pan and let cool. Refrigerate leftovers for the next meal.

Dogs just love the garlic powder, but be sure that it is powder, not garlic salt, that you are using.

Free-Feeding

Some dogs handle free-feeding very well. Many field and working dogs free-feed to keep up the number of needed calories. Many of these dogs have such a high metabolism rate they require a feeding schedule that allows them to refuel constantly. However, unless you see your pup needing this kind of schedule or your vet recommends it, do not rush out to buy a free-feeder at your local pet store. Many owners allow their pups to graze, only to find out later they have an overweight pup. Again, consider the breed of your pup and talk to

A regular feeding schedule will help you to housetrain your puppy, as well as help you to be aware of any health problems your dog may experience.

your vet. While some dogs are naturally lean, others tend to bulk up rather easily.

In the case of Muffin and Edgar, free-feeding was a big issue. Muffin, a sedentary six-year-old chocolate Lab, was about ten pounds overweight. Muffin lived and breathed for the opportunity to snarf up some goody. Edgar, an eleven-month-old Brittany Spaniel, was a competitive runner with his owner. Edgar burned calories in his sleep and bordered on anorexia. So, their owner decided to buy a free-feeder for Edgar.

It was no surprise that Muffin gobbled up all the food, leaving her heavier than ever and Edgar virtually starving. We tried putting the free-feeder outside on the porch. Edgar and the feeder were separated by a screen door from Muffin, the eating machine. That arrangement, or I should say the screen door, lasted one day. Their owner came home to find pieces of kibble strewn across the kitchen floor and hallway. As he approached the porch, he found Muffin lying on her side, only able to thump her tail on the floor and moan. She had ripped her way through the screen door and eaten nearly 20 pounds of dog food!

Edgar was put on a high caloric meal, three times a day, while Muffin's meal was split in half. She was given 1 cup of green beans and 3/4 cup dog food until she dropped some of her weight.

Diet for a Shiny Coat

If your puppy is healthy but has a dull coat or flaking skin, you can add one cup of cottage cheese to his diet to bring back the shine. You may also buy special powders to sprinkle on your pup's food. Dobermans are susceptible to dandruff, so I buy a powder from the pet store to add to Tasha's food. When money is tight, I add a cup of cottage cheese in her food. She likes the cottage cheese better, but the results are pretty similar.

HEARTWORM MEDICINE

It is *very* important that you put your pup on a heartworm preventative plan. Mosquitoes can infect healthy dogs with an infective larvae, an immature heartworm called microfilaria. Once they become adult heartworms, they live in the heart chamber and block proper blood flow, creating a pathological change in the tissues. Your vet can fully explain the medical ramifications of heartworms, but I can assure you they can cause a painful death for your pup. Your vet can run a series of tests on your dog to determine if he has heartworms. As long as he has none, the vet will prescribe a heartworm preventative plan

---

Your dog will need regular checkups to maintain his good health and to prevent any potential problems.

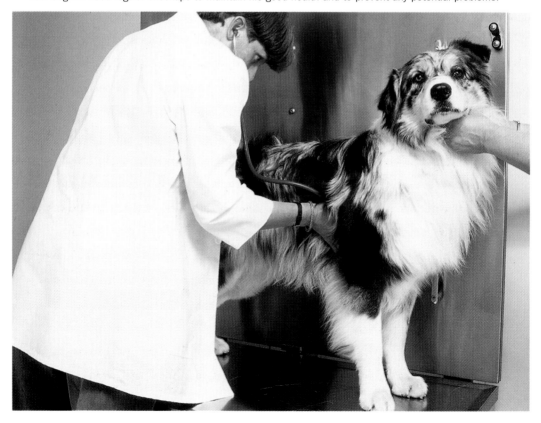

for your dog, which he must be given faithfully. Each dog must test negative *before* being put on the preventative plan. At present, only Arizona and Montana are free of heartworm disease.

FIGHTING FLEAS AND TICKS

There are several important things to know about fleas before you wage war. You must kill the eggs as well as the adults. You must treat your yard as well as your house, and you must use *effective* weapons to fight the fleas. If you do not do all of these things, it will be a long, expensive, and probably futile battle.

Whether you spray or bomb your house for fleas, read the label and be sure that the product guarantees to kill the eggs and adults. If the eggs are able to hatch, you will just have to bomb in another week—a costly and aggravating process.

If you only treat the house, you will find that your puppy will just bring in a new batch of fleas from outside. Unfortunately, cats and squirrels are very big flea carriers. If you can treat your yard once or twice a month, it will help tremendously in the battle against fleas and ticks.

Flea collars are not particularly effective in the control of fleas and ticks for most dogs. The collar will keep the fleas away from the pup's ears, but fleas and ticks will still roam all over the rest of his body. It is better to be sure that you bathe and dip him regularly. Flea and tick dip is the most effective way to control the pests. *Warning!:* Be sure to read the instructions properly when you use dip. Many times the directions call for the dip to be diluted with water. You could make your pup sick if you fail to read the instructions.

Also, here are some helpful bathing tips. Get your pup completely soaked. Lather up your hands and apply the flea and tick shampoo around his neck just below his ears. This is important because when the dog gets wet, the first place the fleas run is into his ears. They can actually hide and survive there during the entire bath. When you shampoo his neck, you are preventing the fleas from moving up.

Next, shampoo his feet. Quickly soap all four. Again, the fleas will try to run and hide in between the pads of his feet. Lather up again and shampoo around his hindquarters. The last place the fleas will try to run before jumping off the dog is his back end. Lather him up all around his tail and hindquarters.

Once you have done this, shampoo the rest of his body. The fleas will have no place to run and will either jump off or die from the chemicals. After he is cleaned, read the directions for the dip and apply it.

Homemade Flea Dip

The ingredients are a half cup of dried rosemary and four cups of boiling water.

Add the rosemary to the water and boil for 20 minutes. Strain and cool. Pour the formula into a spray bottle and spray your pup. Let him completely dry.

Other clients have added one or two tablespoons of brewer's yeast to their puppy's food each night to prevent fleas. It really is effective for many dogs.

Watch for signs of fleas and ticks by checking your dog regularly (daily during the summer). If your pup is scratching and shaking his head, this is an indication that he has fleas. If he does not have fleas, but is scratching and licking his paws constantly, this is a very good sign that he has allergies. Contact your vet about this. There are antihistamines dogs can take; there are also allergy shots for significant allergies that are usually given by veterinary allergists. Your vet can refer you.

TAKING CARE OF YOUR OLDER DOG

As he gets older, your dog is likely to stiffen up, become more finicky with his food, and want to rest more. The result can be that you feel the need to baby him. As much as you want to, this can be a very big mistake. As your dog gets older, it is very important for him to exercise. The amount and intensity of his exercise will decrease, as it does for most older people, but physical activity remains vital to your older dog's health.

Nice, long walks help the circulation and prevent crippling. Walking helps keep your dog's spirits up, his senses sharp, and his body feeling younger. It is easy to think that he wants to lie around all day, but another result of inactivity could be that he becomes depressed.

Most vets recommend bringing another puppy into the house when the first dog starts to get older. I was still in high school when our vet recommended getting a puppy for our 11-year-old dog. At first, Punkin disliked the new puppy, but after several months she warmed up to Tikva and, in the years that followed, they developed a beautiful relationship. They loved each other very much. Punkin became very young and frisky again. Mine is a two-dog family forever. We have seen the love and companionship dogs give each other.

Another mistake we all tend to make is overfeeding our older dogs. We rationalize by saying that he gained weight when he was fixed or he just does not run and play like he used to—and, anyway, he's entitled to some special treatment. The truth is that the older he is, the stiffer his legs will get; so the less extra weight he has to carry, the better. I have seen dogs who are 2 to 4 years younger than my 14-year-old Doberman, but that appear to be

Your older dog may need extra rest, as well as special care and attention, to keep him healthy and comfortable.

older. They are arthritic and encumbered by their weight. Overfeeding your dog is unfair to him. I keep Tasha fit and well-exercised, and I do it for a selfish reason—I want her around forever! If you really love your dog, keep him at his ideal weight.

Destructive Behavior and the Older Dog

The one thing I often hear from owners of older dogs is, "He's forgotten everything! He gets into the trash and ignores me!" Chances are the 15-year-old dog doesn't really care what you have to say about the trash. I've seen some of the best, highest obedience-ranked dogs in the world revert to their puppy ways. The advice that these top handlers have given me as they watched their dogs behavior deteriorate? Moan, sigh, complain loudly, and respect what a great dog you have.

Occasionally, Tasha will let me know if she feels that I have been neglecting her. She will go to the trash can and pull out a tissue, walk up to me, and show me a white tissue tightly clenched between her teeth. She stares deeply and defiantly into my eyes. I will gasp and say, "What are you doing?" First, I will instruct her to drop the tissue, but I know better. What she has planned is for me to try to wrestle it out of her mouth, which I do. I know what she is doing, but she loves it. She has captured *all* of my attention. I am talking to her and touching her. That is all she really wanted in the first place. After our five-minute wrestling match over a used tissue, I tell her what a bad puppy she is and verbally reprimand her. I let a few minutes pass and then, I get on the floor beside her and give her some love. Would I have done this with a two year old? No way. Tasha is 14 years old. She deserves to be humored.

The point is, if your older dog suddenly displays destructive behavior, look for the reason. Has your schedule changed? Has his position in the house been threatened? If he is simply not getting the attention he feels he deserves, increase the training workout or love/hug sessions. Nine times out of ten, that will solve all the problems. (If not, refer to the section on destructive behavior.)

Chances are the biggest problem—not responding to commands, ignoring his name—is that he is going deaf. Every night I let Tasha out at 10:00 before going to bed. We've had this routine for years and years, and yet, I have to go find Tasha and ask her loudly if she wants to go out. When she is barking at the paperboy in the backyard, I have to approach her to tell her to stop barking. She just doesn't hear me anymore. She is not belligerent, just old.

Wetting

When she was about three years old, Tasha began going to the bathroom on her bed. I was shocked that she would do such a thing. Convinced there must be some explanation I did not understand, I asked my vet, who told me that this is common with dogs who have been neutered. There is a chemical imbalance that causes them to lose control of their bladders. They are not even aware of what they have done until they feel the wet spot.

The vet told me that the worst thing I could do was punish her, because the incontinence is a very humiliating occurrence for the dog. After some blood work was done to confirm his diagnosis, he placed Tasha on a weekly medication that has done the trick. Kinder also is incontinent and on a daily medication that controls the problem.

If you have a female or male that suddenly regresses in this way, look for a medical reason before you suspect bad behavior. It is unlikely that after three or four years of good behavior, he will suddenly abandon all rules.

However, if you have a new addition to the family or have changed your normal routine drastically, your dog may be rebelling. Urinating or defecating on the carpet is a sign that he is marking his territory. He may feel threatened by a new pet, child, or mate. He does not like intrusion into his life and wants it known that this is his domain. Treat this as though you would housetraining a puppy. When you catch him committing the act, as it were, push his nose near (very near) the mistake and correct him. Tell him, "Outside," and put him out or walk him. Make sure that it does not turn into playtime. If he goes to the bathroom while you are out, crate him or confine him to a small area. Also, and this is very important, if the

The love, time, and attention you give your dog during training will help to form a strong bond between you.

new person is an adult or older child, include the person in the training. This can create a bond between the new person and the dog and lessen the dog's hostility.

If you have moved to a new house, there is a great chance he is marking his *new* territory. Again, correct him if you can catch him, and confine him while you are gone. In any of these cases, be sure to increase the playtime you spend with him. If you reassure him that nothing has changed between the two of you, he will most likely straighten up. Dogs are very sensitive to their owners. Unfortunately, we are unable to sit them down and explain things to them with mere words. We must show them through our actions.

BONDING WITH YOUR DOG

Playtime is very important to your dog, and research indicates that it is very therapeutic for you, too. Physical contact between you and your dog has calming, reassuring effects on both of you. Play chase, hide-and-seek (a personal favorite of Ziek, my parents' Labrador), and wrestle with your dog. This teaches him to be gentle when he plays with you, and he will love the contact between the two of you.

Playtime is particularly important when you are training. Your pup needs to feel that there is time for training and discipline, but that you always love him no matter what. He will feel comfortable with your hands if you wrestle and tussle with him, but the play should always be gentle. There is nothing more sad than seeing a dog who cringes as he is about to be pet or stroked.

Grooming, as discussed, is an essential part of certain breeds' upkeep. For shorter-coated breeds, it may not be as necessary, but it is still a good idea for all dogs. Regular grooming will not only help you bond with your puppy; it will also assist you in maintaining your dog's health. By brushing and stroking him, you will feel any unusual bumps, lumps, scratches, or abrasions that might otherwise go unnoticed. I once had an Akita student who had a wire lodged in his throat. Upon discovering it, I rushed him to the vet. We determined it had been there for several weeks and had been extremely painful for the pup. His owners had such little physical contact with him, they did not even realize anything was wrong.

Teaching your dog to lie still for grooming not only helps you to make him look good, it also helps you to examine him for any skin or coat problems he may be experiencing.

Additionally, grooming allows you to find ticks and fleas. While ticks do not cause the discomfort to animals that fleas do, they are very dangerous—they are carriers of Lyme disease, which is painful and can be life-threatening. You may find evidence of flea bites on the end of your dog's ears. This is an important discovery because, in addition to the discomfort the actual bite brings, dogs will also violently shake their heads in reaction to the bites, breaking membranes and causing serious long-term damage to themselves. English Cocker Spaniels, for example, must have their ears checks regularly during the summer. Because their long ears hang very close to the ground, they can become host to ticks and burrs, which often cause deafness.

While Tasha was growing up, I made her stand still to be groomed because it got her used to being touched all over. This is very helpful for vets when your dog goes for a checkup. Many dogs jump when they are touched in certain spots. Not Tasha—the dog is a stone. While I bathe her in the backyard, envious neighbors watch as she stands perfectly still until the last rinse is finished. She is also more tolerant of having her nails cut as a result of my touching her. I may pick on my sister for not being a very good disciplinarian (with Kinder; I have to admit that Kaiser is an angel), but I have to give her credit when it comes to grooming. Michelle has a wonderful "touch" relationship with her dogs, and as a result, there are no better dogs than hers at the vet's. Vets have frequently commented on how stoic Kaiser is. Like Tasha, he will stand still for his bath (even come to the hose without being dragged) and to have his nails cut. Kaiser will even allow the vet to brush his great Doberman teeth.

THE LOVE TOUCH

I have talked about the importance of touch with your pet. It builds the relationship of trust, love, and loyalty between the two of you. One of the best ways to create this bond is through massage. Like grooming, it helps the dog to learn to accept being handled, helps you discover any injuries and sensitive areas, and enables you to stay on top of his general health. But, massage is more than that. Your pet will feel love and tenderness through your fingertips. When Tasha was a puppy, I constantly massaged her and rubbed her. As I've mentioned, she allows the vet to do anything with her, and anyone can pet her. Moreover, when I touch her now, 14 years later, she moans and sighs contentedly.

For the young dog, massage offers security and reassurance. Dogs that have come from the pound and/or have been abused or abandoned need this type of touch. Older dogs also need it. It helps their circulation. Stiff joints can be soothed, and knots can be worked out.

Massaging your dog on a regular basis is a great diagnostic activity, and it also allows you to spend quality time bonding with your pet.

To start, begin stroking your dog between his ears on the back of his neck and head. Rub behind each ear and on the jaw muscles. Talk to him while you do this. With a soothing voice, tell him what a good pup he is. Work down the neck. Remember not to press too hard. Rub his shoulders and down each front leg. Play with his toes a little bit. Again, this can help later when you trim his nails. It may help you discover injured paws and fragments caught between his toes. Work your thumbs (together) down his spine. Extend your fingers along his sides as you move down his back. Rub firmly. Stop at his stomach and rub gently. Feel for any lumps or bumps. Work down each hind leg. Run your hands thoroughly down both sides of his leg. Be sure to extend and flex all his legs. This helps the circulation and works out any knots. Rub gently all the way down to the toes. Once I have worked over his body, I will go back to his face and rub him, kiss him, praise him, and scratch his chest and belly for a bit.

As you can well imagine, this offers great diagnostic value as well as real quality time for you and your pup. At the risk of sounding preachy, there is no greater joy than that which comes from the kind of friendship you can build with your dog. Tasha and I are very close. I have figured that, over the years, I have trained several thousand dogs and have boarded nearly two hundred in my home, but she has never been threatened. I have always let her know that she is my one and only Tasha. She knows me so well. She knows tears of pain and tears of joy. When I am depressed, she comes over to me and moans; when I am happy, she wags her little nub at me as though she wants in on it, too; and when I am sick, she jumps up on the bed because she knows I am too weak to push her

There are many things that you can do with your dog that will ensure that you form a partnership that is based on mutual trust, affection, and respect.

off (she's not stupid). She reads me like a book, and I her. I believe that it is only through training, discipline, praise, and quality time that our relationship has developed into something so powerful. I can only hope that everyone can have the kind of relationship with his or her dog that I have tried to share with you in these pages.

LAST THOUGHTS

CELEBRATING YOUR PUP'S BIRTHDAY!

I've been attending dog birthday parties since I was six years old when my Mom invited all the neighborhood dogs to celebrate Punkin's birthday. The day was a huge success as far as canine parties go. There were no fights, everyone kept their hats on, no one fought over the cake, and Punkin got several squeaky toys and a rawhide. That was just the first of 16 birthdays for Punkin. In fact, Punkin, a Beagle/Lab mix, became an old hand at birthdays. We couldn't open those singing cards in the house. Whenever Punkin heard the "Happy Birthday" theme song, it sent her into a delirious cake and ice cream frenzy. Who knew then how our birthday experiences would grow from just three neighborhood dogs in the backyard to sending out invitations and screening suitable guests. But, as any experienced dog-party thrower will tell you, there are necessary precautions.

First, the invitations. Once you have decided on the date and time, be sure to pick out a tasteful invitation. There are a lot of cards depicting dogs in ridiculous positions, wearing clothing, and looking pathetic. Dogs don't think this is funny. Why would they want to attend a party that promises to humiliate them?

Included in the invitation should be an outline of how the day is going to proceed. We all know or, at least, I hope we know that chocolate is toxic for dogs. Offering chocolate cake and chocolate ice cream is not a good idea. Instead, Punkin always insisted upon carrot cake

The author, her dog Punkin, and friends, celebrating one of Punkin's many birthdays.

with a little scoop of vanilla ice cream on the side. However, it is important for your intended guests to know the menu. Many dogs have strict diets or allergies. If that is the case, the owners may bring their own meal or you can prepare something for that special guest.

Whether the dogs bring gifts is up to you, but be sure that every owner understands the guests should arrive on leash. Even the most mild-mannered pup can get carried away with himself at a good canine party. Dogs should be restrained for this reason.

Second, review your guest list. I remember insisting that *all* the neighborhood dogs attend Punkin's party. Even that attack dog down the street. After all, I reasoned, if Punkin was ever going to get along with the foaming, frothing at the mouth German Shepherd, how could she do it if she continued to snub him on her birthday? Dogs are sensitive to these things, and word can get around fast. My mother had the foresight to say, "No."

Inviting two unneutered males, for example, *may* not be such a good idea. The cake, the candles, the singing is all very exciting. Some pups may not be able to handle all the activity like ladies and gentlemen. Cake stealing, snapping, and jumping on the birthday puppy are common responses to such festive activities. Again, this is why it is important to consider who you invite and to be sure that all pups be kept on leash.

The last party that Tasha, Sosi, and I were invited to was for a two-year-old Belgian Shepherd. One of the other guests was Dixie Cupp. (Remember the chocolate Lab that couldn't resist chocolate chip ice cream?) Dixie was beside herself. From the moment she arrived with a doggy bag in the owners' hand, she was out of control. She leapt on top of the other dogs, nearly causing two different fights, and had to be sent outside. When it was time to serve the cake, Dixie was brought inside and put into a down/stay. The cake was brought forward, everyone was singing, tails were wagging, and candles were burning. The Shepherd's owner bent down to show the birthday boy his cake while she sang. She was going to, I assume, blow the candles out for him, when Dixie lost it. She bolted forward and lunged at the cake, burying her nose into the middle of it. She singed her whiskers, the cake flew from the woman's hands, and icing went everywhere. It became a free-for-all, as every dog lunged forward trying to get a piece of cake. We all tried to pull our dog(s) back, but the damage was done. The banana cake was devoured; the birthday was over.

Third, it is always helpful to provide a list of things other owners might need to bring. For example, suggest that owners bring their dogs' dinner bowls. If the weather permits, put each dog's bowl in separate areas of the yard. Once the singing is over, the host can dish a little cake into each bowl. By making the dog lie next to his bowl, you not only keep him out of harm's way from other dogs, but you teach him to wait his turn. It is this kind of patience that will enable your dog to keep his hat on for the duration of the party, thus ensuring future invitations. After all, nobody likes a party pooper.

Some owners may also want to bring their own birthday meal. My sister is a vegetarian and is often forced to do the same thing at barbeques. After the first couple of times, it becomes less embarrassing.

Fourth, the entertainment. Although letting all the dogs run wild in the backyard might seem like a great idea, forget it. Even if you fed them a wheat germ cake, they are still going to be hyped up after the birthday occasion and tempers may flair. Suggest a group walk; maybe certain pups can play in pairs.

Bones, cow hooves, or squeaky toys make good party favors. If cow hooves are passed out, you want to make sure all the dogs are a good distance from each other. What would seem like a great time for the owners to kick back and share a piece of cake could turn ugly in a matter of seconds. That is why long walks or taking turns at a Frisbee™ contest are best.

Finally, remember that the party will probably take eight minutes total, so just have a great time. Don't put a lot of pressure on yourself to decorate. Don't worry about balloons.

Many dogs can live to a ripe old age, and their good health and friendship should be appreciated and celebrated.

Remember that the guests all have very short attention spans and may forget that they actually had cake three seconds after they ate it. At least, that's what they'll try to tell you.

THOUGHTFUL TIPS FOR DOG OWNERS

Consider yourself a lucky person. You have entered the world of pet ownership and can appreciate the joys that your dog gives you that a non-dog owner could never understand. But there are stresses as well. I use my sister as an example. One day while she was visiting me, she looked over and asked, "If something happened to me, would you promise to take and love Kaiser and Kinder?"

I immediately responded, "Of course!" Then, I changed the subject. I didn't want to think about that, but it is something you should consider. Who would take responsibility for your pet if something were to happen to you? He is a living creature who has fears and worries and would not understand your disappearance. For him, your own peace of mind, and his comfort, you must consider this possibility.

Get Well Gifts

How often have you sent a thoughtful card or gift to a friend in the hospital or bedridden at home, but not thought about that person's pet? Most of us don't. But, the most thoughtful thing you can do is offer to care for the pet. If your friend is in the hospital, perhaps you can arrange to stay in the house and care for the dog or cat. Knowing that one's pet is being taken care of will increase the chances of a speedy recovery. The patient will have peace of mind and be able to rest properly. If you are unable to stay in the house, perhaps you and a group of friends could pitch in and have a sitter service stay with the pet.

Pet Gifts for a Friend

What if you have an invitation to a canine birthday party? What are you going to give the birthday pup? There are several dog catalogs that have great gifts for dog lovers. (You'll find a variety of catalogues offered in dog magazines.) You can order dog beds, bones, rubber toys, nylon bones, specialized collars, leashes, and dog bowls. You can buy stationary or note pads with a favorite breed on it for the human in the pair.

Other great gift ideas are a year's supply of dog biscuits or a donation in your friend's name to the Humane Society. You might get a picture of your friend's dog without him/her knowing it and have it enlarged and framed. Or you can hire an artist to paint a portrait. Gifts featuring pets are always winners.

REPORTING NEGLECT

On a much more serious note, if you even *suspect* abuse to an animal, report it to the animal control people in your area. Call the police or the ASPCA (American Society for Prevention of Cruelty to Animals). The ASPCA is a successful lobbying group that has fought to ensure protection laws for animals.

If you see a stray running loose in the neighborhood, do not be afraid to call animal control. We have images of the "dog catcher" as being the bad guy, but what could be worse than the dog being hit by a car or being hungry, cold, and afraid. Many times, dogs do not die quickly, but suffer slow, painful deaths. The animal control people offer a warm, dry area with food and water. That is far better treatment than the streets offer. Make the call.

BECOMING A RESPONSIBLE PET OWNER

In my group classes, I demonstrate for my students how the typical dog owner, all too often, behaves. I have my human students put their dogs in down/stays, and then I lead another dog very close to theirs. I let my dog trample around their dogs while I engage in conversation. I pretend that I assume their dogs are as friendly as mine and almost let them touch noses. I annoy the other people and, sometimes, the dogs. I am being, I am afraid to say, the typical dog owner.

Too often, I see people take their dogs to the park and let them off lead even when other dogs are present. Their defense: "My dog is very friendly." What is never considered is that the other dog(s) may not be. I have seen too many dog fights result from such a lack of

Dog ownership is a big responsibility. You, as an owner, are in charge of your pet's health, safety, and well-being throughout your life together.

thoughtfulness. When you are walking your dog and decide to let him off lead, look around. If there are other dogs there, bring him back in. Owners of "friendly" breeds are very guilty of this. For example, Labs are such friendly animals, it never occurs to their owners that some people may be deathly afraid of large dogs (or any dogs), or that the dog on the other side of the field may be extremely aggressive. Many people own aggressive dogs that they are unable to control. Amazing, but true. Be responsible. Your friendly pup does not know any better, but you do!

People who own small dogs tend to let them roam around off lead, often wandering up to other larger dogs. These same people would think twice if they were aware of how many dogs I have trained who have tried to kill or have succeeded in killing small dogs, and I am only one trainer. Even more disturbing, the smaller dogs are very often the aggressor, showing signs of aggression toward larger dogs. Not smart, but true. All dogs should remain on a lead while they are in public. For the safety of you, your pup, and others, be a responsible owner. Not everyone is as fortunate as you and I in having and knowing well-trained, well-behaved dogs. Please be careful and courteous.

THE FINISHING LINE

Y ou have done a lot of work. You have read the book, trained your dog, and learned a lot about yourself and your pet. This is quite an accomplishment. Do not let everything go. Reinforcement is the key to keeping your sanity intact and your puppy happy. In keeping with my storytelling, I have yet one more.

I have mentioned already how my parents' nutty dog, Ziek, went berserk when anyone left the house. Even though he had gone through all his training and, in general, was a great dog, he still became hysterical if anyone left the house. He barked and shrieked. So, we worked on long stays to help him with self-control. Now, he picks up a stuffed toy in his mouth to stifle his cries. Besides being very cute, it works. However, my mother has a friend who loves to come over and rile Ziek into hysterics. Mom protests that Ziek only behaves this way with one person. Not true. He tries it with everyone, except we immediately correct him and he grabs his toy. The point is: As long as even one person undermines the training, the dog will always believe there is a chance to try with someone else.

Remember the important rules to being a successful handler? You must make sure that you are communicating properly with your dog. You must make all your actions clear and be sure that you are not sending confusing messages. Be sure that you are consistent and that you always praise good behavior.

Providing your pup with positive reinforcement and regular refresher lessons is the key to your dog displaying consistent and reliable behavior.

REFRESHER LESSONS

Be sure once you have finished training your dog that you don't throw away the book and think you and your dog will never need refresher lessons. When Taffy, a young male blonde Cocker Spaniel, graduated from basics, Mr. and Mrs. P. were concerned that he might regress after some time. Their concerns were valid. Once the training course is over, few dog owners continue to work their dog. Within a few weeks, their pup may go back to pulling the lead and jumping up and down on people. Exasperated, the owners will return to class only to find that the dog has not forgotten one thing. The owners did. The owners stopped enforcing the heel or the stay and forgot to give the okay command frequently so that their dog began to break training whenever he felt like it. After one lesson, it is almost always apparent who forgot what.

In the case of Taffy, his owners are an older couple who, both suffering from back injuries, are slow to correct. Taffy knows this and is prone to bully them a bit. For those who have a more stubborn or aggressive dog, the workouts should not stop. You do not need to work your dog every day as you have in the past weeks, but once or twice a week is needed to maintain good, reliable behavior. In situations similar to this, the owners should involve a third person in the training. When both owners are having back difficulties, they can rely on a third person to enforce Taffy's training. This will prevent Taffy from getting sloppy or trying to test her owners with negative behavior.

If time has slipped away from you (and it does), there is no reason to start all over again. Even if it has been over a year (*but please don't let this happen*), your pet will remember his paces—you just need to give him a little jump start. Start with the heel command as you

With basic obedience training, who knows how far you and your dog can go? Organized dog events and sports are just some activities in which you and your pet can participate.

learned it, the automatic sit at the curbs or every time you stop, and the stay and down commands. Once your pup appears to be in the swing of things, try the recall and stays from a greater distance. You may need to refer again to the "How to Give a Proper Correction" section of the book.

I have found that with refresher lessons, it takes about three workouts before both owner and dog are just where they left off. The owner is always more awkward than the pup. Dogs have wonderful memories; they love the attention, the exercise, and the work. This is another reason why you should never let too much time go between the workouts. It is unfair to your pet. A good workout is truly a treat for dogs. As busy as I have been at times, I try to do something special for Tasha, Nala, and Sosi once a week, and the best part is how we all feel once it's over. They smile and plop next to me in a heap, panting and content, and I feel happy that I have done something for them.

And, one more time, I have to ask you these questions: While you work your pup, are you watching that left hand? Are you telling him "okay" before you end the lesson? Are you praising him consistently? Are you using body language and verbal tones to let him know what it is you want? Are you repeating commands to him so that he knows both the verbal and physical commands? If you have answered "yes" to all of these questions and you are doing it more than 90 percent of the time, you have passed with flying colors.

I wish you as much happiness with your pal as I've had with mine over the years. Good luck!

GRADUATION DAY

Early one Saturday morning, we gathered in the parking lot of the county recreation center. Lined in front of me were two Basset Hounds, two Cockers, one Golden, one Dalmatian, one Keeshond, one Boxer, two black Labradors, two mixed breeds, one Sheltie, one Gordon Setter, one Newfoundland, and one Border Collie.

This was a special class; this was the big day. It was Graduation Day and everyone was on his or her best behavior. As the class began with owners heeling their dogs in circles, I heard many of the owners telling their dogs, "You'd better watch it! She's watching you." Someone muttered, "This is your big day, buddy. Don't blow it."

The pups had no idea it was a special day. They pranced and trotted around, pretending to ignore each other like it was any other training session. We did our downs, automatic sits, stays, and recalls. We switched owners and dogs. We trotted, ran, and dragged our feet. The people threw balls around to each other while the dogs were in downs or sit/stays. (This was particularly taxing for the Labs.) I teased the dogs with liver treats. I stood five feet away from dogs in their down/stays and cooed, "Oh, he's a pretty baby. Oh, I just love to give big puppy hugs." They squirmed, wagged, and whined, but not one budged. This was the finest group of canine/human couples I had ever worked with. Each owner was very serious about improving life with his or her furry friend.

It was the owners who were sweating bullets. As I stood there with my clipboard, I am

All the hard work and effort you put into training your dog will pay off with a happier, well-adjusted pet and lots of new friends to help you celebrate.

sure they thought I was grading them. I wasn't. They had already made the grade. I was looking over the information sheets each owner had filled out on our first meeting. I looked at Sandy the Sheltie's sheet. His owner, 12-year-old Chris, had written that he wanted to "tame and teach my dog. I wish to make him a companion with a high level of obedience." I watched Chris for a few moments. He and Sandy walked in perfect unison between big 'ol Rufus, the Newfoundland, and Ace, the Labrador. Sandy paid them very little attention now. The first class, Sandy had nearly passed out when Rufus walked by.

Taffy, the Cocker, marched by at a much slower pace. When Mr. P.'s Parkinson's disease progressed, Mrs. P. took over the lessons. But Mr. P. was there, watching as Taffy worked through the crowd with his downs, sits, and stays. He heeled beautifully next to his mistress, accepting the slower pace. In answer to the question about what he expected from this course, Mr. P. had written simply, "how to control my dog." He had described Taffy as "hyperactive." I was very pleased with this threesome. Because they had practiced so much with long stays, Taffy had really learned to control himself. As he had matured, he had learned he could not pull his owners and settled into their slow pace. During our first classes, Taffy had actually tried to take on the Labs and Golden that outweighed him by 50 pounds. Now, he completely ignored them.

I smiled as Ace traipsed by. As he passed me, he had to poke out his long nose and give me a quick nudge. "See? See?" he was saying. I flipped through my papers and found Denise and Ace. Describing Ace's behavioral problems, Denise had written, "He screeches at me and jumps." He was a screeching, jumping lunatic when we first met. But Denise did an amazing job and remains one of the best students I've ever had. Her determination and dedication were undaunted even as Ace leaped, screeched, and leaped. Now, I was looking at one of my future off-leash students.

Pepper, the Border Collie, and Ms. H. walked by. Ms. H. had asked that she have a dog "that obeys always and from a distance, too." It was Graduation Day and by all accounts, Pepper was a rock. Once she was in a sit/stay or down/stay, little could make her move. Her recalls were poetry in motion, but the most wonderful thing about Pepper was how she watched Ms. H. while they worked. The admiration and respect she had for Ms. H. could not be missed. We had already begun the first steps of off-leash training with Pepper, who was taking commands more than 20 feet away, and the two of them were ready to move on to a whole new level of training. Ms. H. had gotten everything she asked for and more.

In the middle of the giant circle lay Max, the Golden. Marilyn flipped and tugged on his leash and teased him with a squeaky toy. Max did not budge. Marilyn and Max, too, were ready for off-leash training. Like Denise and Ms. H., Marilyn had invested a great deal of time and love in the training, and it showed in her pup. Stepping farther away, through the maze of puppies, Marilyn raised her left hand straight out, signaling the recall command. She didn't say a word. On her information sheet, she had asked, "Is it possible that he will come when called?" As Marilyn raised her hand, Max scrambled to his feet, trotted through the other dogs, avoiding Taffy and Ace, and performed a perfect recall, sitting at his mistress' side.

Finally, weaving through the crowd was big Rufus. The class bully. The class clown. The puppy voted "Least Likely to Succeed" by his classmates. As Clay heeled him past me, Rufus cut eyes at me to see if I was watching. He was showing off. Recently, he had turned into a bit of a showoff, loving the attention and positive reinforcement of basic obedience. I grinned. "Clay, have him do a series of downs," I said. Clay nodded. Rufus had always hated having to go down, then sit, then down again, over and over, as we demanded of him. Everyone watched as Rufus obliged without the slightest grumble.

"Okay, last test," I called out. "Before they can graduate, they have to wear these for a picture!" I pulled out mortar boards I had made to fit the puppy heads. The owners half

This Lab and owner proudly accept their diploma for their great accomplishment.

With a strong foundation in basic obedience behind him, who knows how far your canine friend can go?

laughed, half groaned. But, one by one, owners placed the elastic bands under the pups' chins and told them to stay. Last but not least was Rufus. For fun, I added, "And everyone has got to wear one. It's all for one here." Clay didn't appreciate that, but sternly told Rufus to stay as he placed the mortar board on Rufus' giant head. Rufus stayed.

"Congratulations!" I said, and several owners ripped the puppies' caps off and tossed them into the air. (Which caused most of the dogs to attack the caps.) But, Clay kept his. He was leaning over talking in Rufus' ear. I couldn't hear what he was saying, but there was no missing Rufus' tail. It was wagging mightily while Clay hugged his pup. Later, I looked at Clay's information sheet to see what he had written in answer to the question, "What do you expect from this course?" Clay had written simply: "A happier dog."

Mission accomplished.

INDEX

PHOTO CREDITS

Alexandra Powe Allred: 12, 13, 25, 51, 52, 53, 68, 69, 70, 72, 73, 76, 80, 82, 83, 84, 85, 87, 90, 92, 93, 95, 96, 98, 100, 119, 160, 181, 183, 195, 202, 214, 216

Isabelle Francais: 19, 20, 21, 22, 24, 27, 28, 29, 31, 33, 34, 35, 38, 39, 40, 44, 54, 55, 56, 60, 61, 62, 66, 67, 71, 102, 103, 105, 107, 109, 112, 116, 117, 118, 120, 122, 124, 128, 129, 131, 136, 140, 141, 143, 145, 147, 149, 150, 153, 155, 157, 158, 159, 162, 165, 169, 170, 173, 176, 180, 186, 187, 189, 190, 193, 196, 199, 206, 210, 211

Alan Leschinski: 57, 172, 198

Liz Palika: 59, 75, 125, 151

Alice Pantfoeder: 41, 43

Robert Pearcy: 204